The Watchman

The Watchman

‹‹

C. EDWARD HOPKIN

Thomas Y. Crowell Company
NEW YORK · ESTABLISHED 1834

The Biblical quotations in this book are taken from the Revised Standard Version unless otherwise indicated.

PREFACE

To a group of clergy gathered annually at Kent, Connecticut, I owe the initial impulse to express the germinal ideas of *The Watchman,* and to the Thomas Y. Crowell Company encouragement and guidance in developing them for publication. My wife, Ruth Kennell Hopkin, contributed much of the manuscript typing and many suggestions. I alone am responsible for all surviving defects.

It is my earnest hope that, in addition to the Episcopal clergy, those of other disciplines may find these pages useful.

C. EDWARD HOPKIN

The Divinity School of the Protestant
Episcopal Church in Philadelphia
June, 1959

CONTENTS

Son of man, I have made thee a watchman unto the house of Israel: therefore hear the word at my mouth, and give them warning from me.

(EZEKIEL 3:17)

INTRODUCTION

In the Ordinal of *The Book of Common Prayer* the Bishop is directed to deliver to those to be ordained an exhortation containing the following words: "And now again we exhort you, in the Name of our Lord Jesus Christ, that ye have in remembrance, into how high a Dignity, and to how weighty an Office and Charge ye are called: that is to say, to be Messengers, Watchmen, and Stewards of the Lord; to teach, and to premonish, to feed and provide for the Lord's family; to seek for Christ's sheep that are dispersed abroad, and for his children who are in the midst of this naughty world, that they may be saved through Christ for ever."

It is clear that as "messengers" they are "to teach," and that as "stewards" they are "to feed and provide for the Lord's family." As "watchmen," however, they are "to premonish," that is, to exercise the prophetic function of warning people against the destructive currents of thought in their environment.

When we think over this charge to be watchmen of the Lord, it turns out to be a fearful command. The stately language of the Prayer Book and the polite obsolescence of that word "premonish" conceal a dangerous function. It is as though the front-line troops received an order to advance, written on vellum and illuminated. For the Christian clergy the order re-

quires them to be something different from the popular, stereo-
typed pattern. The "parson" is, in most people's eyes, what the
derivation of the word implies, the person of the community.
Can he criticize and still be thus accepted? Again, the "pastor"
is, in most people's eyes, the one who sees some good in every-
body. Can he denounce and still be the pastor? If he does denounce, is he right or wrong?

Nor do the dangers undergone by a watchman consist only
in the jeopardizing of his personal popularity. If he is married,
as a husband he merges his self with that of another; children
extend his forgetfulness of self for the sake of others, and they
bring additional obligations. Yet still he is engaged in the dangerous role of watchman. As a pastor he identifies himself with
a much larger spiritual family, again with no change in his
watchman's duties. Though he may write off a threat to his
personal prestige, he cannot blithely ignore the suffering his
family may have to endure in the event of his loss of esteem or
salary. Nor can he blindly enter upon a career of public criticism without considering how far he should risk the spiritual
welfare and peace of his congregation.

In sharp contrast to the situation of the generality of Protestant ministers is that hard-hitting watchman at the opening of
the Gospel story, John the Baptist. How appropriate it seems
to us that he should have been a man disciplined to personal
discomfort, free of family obligations, and free, also, of the task
of being the pastor of a congregation. From the vantage ground
of these freedoms he spoke incisively. So deeply did he cut
through the crust of human complacency that he actually drew
hearers, it would appear, in direct proportion to the bitterness
of his words. He exposed truth so nakedly, and the people
wanted this truth so hungrily, that though he spoke from the

wilderness they came out to him. No stained-glass windows, nor Gothic towers, nor trained choirs were there to help him. His drawing-card was his theme—the Kingdom of God.

Let us be honest. Most of us of the clergy cannot step into the niche of John the Baptist. God gives that place to a very few. Nor do we convey John's message well merely by shouting more loudly. Moreover, were we to assess our tasks with truth, we would deem ourselves already submerged by the functions of messenger and steward, before turning to that of watchman. Only Jesus Christ carried all three roles perfectly. The impossibility of the tasks laid on us makes us, then, religious. That is to say, we should rather resign and go into secular work than be watchmen without God.

Yet this reveals another obstacle to the carrying out of the command. Messengers, watchmen, and stewards without God we are bound to be if some curb is not put on the demands which a church makes on its pastor. He must visit, he must organize, he must preach, he must represent the church in the community, and he must share as well in the social life of his congregation. Up to a point, the heavy burdens of these composite demands may drive him to the sustenance of prayer. But let the pressures become too great and the would-be watchman can no longer be God's watchman, for he no longer has the time for prayer and communion with God. He is merely the exhausted servant of a deceptive schedule of activities, religious by intention but piously worldly in fact. The pastor who likes it may gain, for himself, success. The pastor who does not like it may be broken by it. Neither will serve the purposes of God.

We clergy know these facts, even when we do not confess our knowledge publicly. We know that the function of moral prophecy is a dangerous one, both for ourselves and for those we love. Sometimes, therefore, we neglect it out of fear; but we also, at other times, rush into it unprepared, urged on, it may be, by the very danger of the requirement.

I knew a clergyman who exemplified the latter course of action. He was, in fact, unmarried. His pastoral relations with his people were excellent and his character of the highest order. One day he was called upon to minister to a child dying of pneumonia. The child and family were previously unknown to him, so it was with shocked surprise that he found them living in a tenement with one partition partially missing, and with structural decay so extensive that both privacy and warmth were virtually impossible. Inquiry revealed that one of his own vestrymen was the owner of the building and the landlord of the family in question. Fired to righteous fury, the clergyman preached on the subject from the pulpit, found himself involved in an altercation with the vestryman after the service and, before long, looking for another parish.

Was it wrong for this pastor to denounce what he saw? Assuming that his knowledge of the facts was reasonably accurate, he found in the church itself a godless unconcern for human misery; therefore we can hardly call him wrong in the substance of his action. Was his sacrifice a fruitless one? No, because the witness afforded by his action remained in the memory of the community. Did he employ the right methods throughout? Unfortunately, he did not. Some of the force of his prophetic action was lost by the altercation after service, in which the vestryman was more adept and convincing. Had he not made some mistakes of procedure, it is probable that the good result would have been much greater, from the standpoint of his work as messenger and steward, as well as from the standpoint of his work as a watchman of the Lord.

It is clear, then, that more is required of us than the development of noble characters. We must take time to cultivate our communion with God. The activities of the church, including the pastor's natural love of people, must give way to this communion. Only God can work in us that which is well pleasing in his sight.

It is also clear that we cannot be the Lord's watchmen without giving thought to ourselves as his servants, to the development of our ability to act as his instruments, instead of as the instruments of our temperamental impulses.

We must also move outside ourselves and observe the world around us from a religious standpoint. We must reject the temptation to view the environment from the angle of personal or even of ecclesiastical success. What is required of us is that we scrutinize modern life from the standpoint of its effects upon God's people and upon their relation to God.

It is the purpose of this book to encourage and abet the minister to greater effectiveness in his role as watchman. The several chapters will deal primarily with the two important foundations of the watchman's competence touched upon briefly above: his relationship to God as his servant (Part One), and his outlook upon the contemporary world, especially as it affects Christianity in America (Part Two).

PART ONE

‹‹

Means & Methods

Chapter 1

THE NEED FOR PREPARATION

Why should the watchman prepare? If preparation is necessary, of what does it consist?

These are questions raised by the Ordinal's exhortation, "that ye have in remembrance, into how high a Dignity, and to how weighty an Office and Charge ye are called." Some of us plunged into pastoral work—let us confess it—not remembering these words of exhortation, and hence, to our sorrow, not asking the appropriate questions. Our mistakes bore witness to our neglect.

This chapter intends to help others who are more prudent forestall a similar damage within their ministries.

1 THE HUMAN MORAL SCENE

At first sight it does not appear that a great amount of preparation is required for being a watchman. The readiness with which we level moral judgments at one another makes prophetic announcement look quite easy. Furthermore, our impressions seem to be backed up by the methods of no less than John the Baptist. The simplicity of his specified requirements is disarming. When the multitudes asked him, "What then shall we do?" he answered, "He who has two coats, let him share with him who has none; and he who has food, let him do likewise."

When the tax collectors asked the same question he said, "Collect no more than is appointed you." His prescription for the soldiers was, "Rob no one by violence or by false accusation, and be content with your wages." [1] Nothing could be simpler.

It is a common pitfall to assume in one's daily living that moral decision is as simple as that. Either on this assumption, or on emotional impulse, we judge one another at home, at work, and in church. We judge ourselves morally in the same manner. Then to our serious dismay the matter of judgment turns out not to be simple at all. It is possible to spend a lifetime never emerging from the condemnation of self; and to exchange judgments with the most responsible adversary without ever reaching a common grasp of the truth which each thought so obvious. Our typical experience is one of moral frustration.

Most of us have the impression that this frustration began sometime in childhood and that it has grown worse with the advancing years. Not that in childhood we did what was right. We may have behaved badly. But our judgments of right and wrong had an assured simplicity. With the increase of experience this assured simplicity was exchanged for a wait-and-see complexity. The change was subtle. Only by hindsight can we thus describe it. At the time it felt as though we were growing up; that is, we thought we were exchanging a foolish notion of right and wrong for one which was more socially approved, and therefore better. Hence we slipped from assurance to uncertainty with the passage of the years.

For a few adults, the graph of moral assurance and certainty can be seen to rise again later, some of the assured simplicity returning as life draws toward its close. These are the

---

[1] Luke 3:10 ff.

ones who have had so much experience with socially approved judgments that they have ceased to regard them as sacrosanct, but who nevertheless, by some spiritual resource, have managed to remain co-operative members of society.

Other adults are not able to achieve this state of independent co-operation. It is characteristically a distant goal, seldom reached. The far more typical states are those of moral frustration for the conscientious and of confused indifference for the others. These color the society to which we are accustomed.

Because the human scene is morally confused, Jesus said, "Judge not, that you be not judged," [2] and he characterized the Pharisees as "blind guides." [3] He seemed to think it normal that people who wanted the kingdom of God would have to ask, seek and knock, until the object of desire was obtained.[4] He described the gate that leads to life as a narrow one, and the way a hard one, which only a few find.[5]

And if we reread the story of John the Baptist's preaching, it becomes evident that the very plainness of his answers reflected the moral confusion of the multitudes, the tax collectors, and the soldiers. Had they not been confused, they would not have needed this moral specialist to help them distinguish such simple rights and such simple wrongs.

2   THE WATCHMAN'S DILEMMA

The concept of a watchman evokes the image of a man in a tower, or placed in some other favorable position which enables him to see what other people cannot. Free association would hardly lead one to picture him as one of the throng in a

---

[2] Matthew 7:1.   [3] Matthew 15:14.   [4] Matthew 7:7.   [5] Matthew 7:14.

busy street, least of all the person who is hurrying most. Yet, when we clergy emerge from ordination we are quite naturally in a hurry, and in proportion as success results from our labors we continue to be in a hurry. There is about this a normal participation in the life immediately confronting us. Within reason, and assuming certain valid goals, such activity is a constructive necessity in the ministry. However, it does not comport with being a watchman, for it robs us of the lookout post.

Activity and hurry entail involvement in the confused moral scene. Wrong behavior is everywhere, as is also the social acceptance of wrong behavior, an acceptance which makes wrong appear right. Therefore, merely to build a church building and to gather into it a bustling congregation, happy in the fact that they all have similar cultural interests, economic resources, and political aims, is simply to grant religious privileges without any religious requirements.

Happily no congregation presents such a worldly aspect totally, but neither is any congregation free from it. In the very activity whereby he does his work, the clergyman participates in the blindness of the world. This immoral quality which floods the Church does not appear on the surface. It is of the very nature of the world to promise one thing while doing another, and to keep its real policies concealed. Thus it becomes "unwise" to welcome certain kinds of people to church, or to let conviction ever displace charm of personality.

It is all too easy to lay upon the clergyman the charge of becoming a watchman, to read to him the exhortation from the Ordinal of *The Book of Common Prayer,* to tell him to "buck up," "be a man," "stand for God and for the right." Many a pastor has anticipated such a "fight talk," in fact has tried to assume the watchman's role. Then the troubles began, no doubt, nor were they constructive.

No idealistic clergyman who has found himself in this situation and who has bravely tried to stand for moral truth would ever care to recall the needless, purposeless humiliations which followed. In so far as courage was rewarded by some good consequence, most would testify that the good came from the hand of God rather than from the courage itself. When, on the other hand, the brave prophet was revealed as factually wrong; when his own character failed to stand up under the resulting counterattack, and when the persons criticized had at their disposal a more subtle and convincing technique of public relations, then the watchman was, in truth, unready for his task.

To be sure, these experiences are closely related to what Jesus meant by the "cross," because the cross was an instrument whereby a violated society thought to rid itself of the violator, and the defeated watchman was, in a sense, bearing this cross. Yet more careful consideration shows that Jesus' cross-bearing was a prepared and selected one. It was not indiscriminate. He did not rush to his cross before accomplishing the rest of his mission, and when he did submit to the death of the cross it was with such worldwide effect as to surpass in its impact every other deed of history.

Jesus must have had this principle of preparation and selection partly in mind when he said to his followers, "Behold, I send you out as sheep in the midst of wolves; so be wise as serpents and innocent as doves." [6]

[6] Matthew 10:16 ff.

3 CAUSES OF THE DILEMMA

Once the causes of the watchman's unreadiness are identified, then something can be done toward removing them. The three most important causes are the lack of factual knowledge germane to complex moral situations, the unconscious personal involvement of the watchman himself in the moral confusion of society, and the subtle skill of the perpetrators of evil.

The first of these, lack of factual knowledge, is illustrated by the unhappy experience of a rural pastor who took occasion to denounce the injustice of certain court procedures in a nearby large city. A clergyman of deep sympathy with the underprivileged, his work with them had given him contacts with the inmates of the county prison. Thinking himself safely in the right, he voiced before a church group severe criticisms of the manner in which court cases were tried in a chronological order juggled in such a way as to be favorable to those of the accused who enjoyed political backing. To his discomfort, the criticism was carried to the presiding judge, who immediately called upon the clergyman to substantiate the charge. Unable to do so, he was maneuvered into making a public apology, although still reasonably convinced he was right.

As our civilization grows more and more complex, the problem of judging the rights and wrongs of public issues becomes increasingly difficult. Knowledge of the facts is essential. This may require long research as well as a method of obtaining hidden information. To most of us this kind of information is not available, and if it were we might not have the freedom and the ability to gather it. The watchman for the concrete situations of public affairs is almost bound to become a specialist. If he is God's specialist, and speaks with the spiritual conviction and resources of a religious man, he performs a most needed task.

The second cause for the watchman's dilemma is his own moral imperfection, which he shares with humanity. This is part of what the Church means by original sin. No one of us has emerged into his adult life with the singleness of eye to see things as they really are. The subtleties of this inward condition defy expression in concrete terms. We know them by their consequences in our outlook and behavior. Since the watchman is entering upon a highly dangerous task, full of tension, and is opening the door to antagonistic relationships, his own spiritual imperfections will reveal themselves damagingly.

This does not mean that we must wait to be perfect before administering a rebuke, but it does impose two cautions. First, the rebuke is a directive rather than a judgment. Second, the watchman is prone to spoil the work if he attempts it without deeply searching prayer, or allows his unredeemed impulses to control his conduct. The display of temper, the overstated charge, and the hasty decision are ever present dangers.

The third cause, the superior maneuvering ability of the perpetrators of evil, is a phenomenon which people of good will discover slowly and painfully through much experience. The clergyman who gives himself trustingly to others is no match for the worldling. Whether it be the domination of church policies by a powerful few within the congregation, or the operations of a vice ring in the community, the person of good will needs vast wisdom before he can act decisively and with good effect.

Of these three causes of the watchman's dilemma, the first can be met by intellectual discipline and diligence. Once cautioned, we will remember never to enter into serious criticism of concrete public situations without possession of the supporting facts. Even though it may not be possible to garner them all, it is still a rule that a moral warning must stay within the limits of what the watchman can support by sure, evidential knowledge.

The cure for the second and third causes is not so quickly stated. Personal involvement in society's blindness and the inability to deal with worldlings are so deeply psychological that they must find their answer not just in an intellectual discipline, but in a spiritual discipline.

Chapter 2

THE PREPARATION

1 THE LOST IMAGE

The Christian's answer to the problem of moral confusion is the doctrine of the image of God. Since man's life is personal, dynamic, and organic, good and evil are personal, dynamic, and organic. Therefore it is only by a rough approximation, resulting in an unsatisfactory makeshift, that we draw lists of right things to do and wrong things to do. Such lists are necessary because morals must occasionally be thought about, and we have to stop the flow of personal life in order to be able to think about it; but the good life is more than the good list. If we want a foundation for what is good, we must have a really personal foundation. The Bible gives us this in the Person of God. Good is good because it is the way God acts and wills us to act. Evil is evil because it is contrary to God's action and will. It follows as a corollary that, since God is the source of life, good is favorable to life and evil destroys life.

If good derives from God, how is it that we have such a concern about good and evil, seemingly from within ourselves? Even the world's most wicked people make a great play for the good, pretending to have it when they do not. Moreover, in our most morally frustrated moments we seem driven by an inward compulsion to act as though we were intensely moral. Philosophers have devised various explanations for this hunger which man has for morals, but Christianity explains it very simply by the statement that God makes man in his own image. That is, the creature is endowed with some of the personal nature of the Creator, and from this endowment comes that intuition that good goes together with life and life with good.

But the image is lost from view. Something has happened to keep it from functioning, with the result that evil masquerades as good, and good is often misunderstood as evil. It is the watchman who points this out. He is the one who, however imperfectly, has recovered for himself a sufficient sight of the image to enable him to distinguish the real good from its imitations, to denounce the false and to proclaim the true. Since he is, of himself, incapable of this role, he must wait for the conditioning, the equipment and, most of all, the command.

2   GOD ENTERS

If God, like the list of morals, could be represented by a diagram, He would be only a most interesting object of human inquiry. But God is the Person from whom all life is derived. He purposely waits to be invited. Then, when he is invited, he enters in response to the watchman's plea for help. If he is to find answers to his dilemma, the watchman must first meet a double prerequisite: he must believe in the active God, and he must confess his own helplessness. This is a reversal of the usual order. Most of us discover, through failure, the fact of our helplessness, and then we take the step of prayer. Yet, men and women do not take the second step of prayer if they have no hope.

Hope is not just a subjective feeling. It has a base in, it comes from, the God believed in, the God who acts. Prayer is the application of this hope, in faith.

Here enter the dual requirements of love and truth. Since God is not indifferent, I can have relations with him only on his terms of love and truth. At that point the problem of my incompetence begins to be solved, in principle, because the God who requires the impossible must also be the One to supply what he requires. If there is hatred or falsehood in me too deep to be eradicated at a stroke, this God accepts me on the basis of my desire. What he asks of me is the hunger and thirst, not the achievement nor the knowledge. He provides the results in his own way and time.

This leads us to an undistorted view of religious prophecy. It now becomes clear why the Book of Ezekiel speaks of the "watchman *unto the house of Israel.*" [1] Only the house of Israel can have this kind of watchman, the kind, that is, who is God-directed and who even has the words put into his mouth by Jehovah. Other societies have other types of watchmen. The Soviets have theirs and the democracies have theirs. Each local community likewise has its kind of watchman. All these latter types are watchmen under the compulsion of a human community afraid of losing control.

The watchman of the house of Israel is equally under compulsion, but he is not under the compulsion of a power afraid of losing control. God has created a universe in which chance blends with predictability and freedom with compulsion. On one level of our perception we can say that he never thinks of control because he does not have to. On another level we can say that he purposely withdraws from controlling his creatures because he has certain high ends in which he wants

---

[1] Ezekiel 3:17.

them to share. He doesn't prevent war, or forcibly bend man to his will, because that kind of compulsion is not within his scheme of things. In no case does he act from fear, as must the human community.

Being, then, the servant of this God, the future watchman learns to take every step from a background of prayer. Because prayer is most naturally stimulated by need, it is practiced most often in distress. On the other hand, the clergyman is in no position to follow the lame procedure of rushing ahead in self-confidence when all goes well and reserving his prayers for times of trouble. It is important to remember our need when we are not feeling it, just as much as when we are feeling it. If prayer always waits for the crisis, the lesson of humility has been badly learned. "Lead us not into temptation, but deliver us from evil" [2] is a petition which Jesus taught his followers with the sunshine periods in mind rather than those of crisis. Consolation and refreshment we all need, but their by-product of self-confidence is no diet for a watchman. On the contrary, it is wonderful to see how much God helps those who pray before the emergency, before the temptation, before the crisis; that is to say, before it is even foreseen. Every crisis well met because well prepared for is a step in the direction of being a good watchman.

3   SELF-ACCEPTANCE

On the one side is God and his activities toward me. On the other side is myself. Sharing the general confusion of the human race into which I was born, and having added to the

[2] Matthew 6:13.

confusion by my own sin, I really do not know myself. Sincere, let us hope, in my conscious life, I may yet be full of darkness within, facing a long road of shocks and humiliations before I can hope to enjoy that soundness of eye whereby my whole body will be full of light.[3]

Here we must stop to check the kind of acceptance we give to this fact. Accept ourselves we must, in one way or another, in order to live. The question remains whether our self-acceptance will be of the true or the false variety.

The question is troublesome because it is my own darkness which I am trying to see, but it is also my own darkness which keeps me from seeing. Yet there is a way out, as long as I keep in mind the two ingredients, God and myself, in actual situations.

Our hope is based upon the fact that it is the real me upon whom God acts. He does not take me out of myself and out of my situations, but rather works on me as I actually am and in my current situations. Perhaps the analogy is helpful here of those small models of sailing vessels which their makers insert somehow into bottles, to be exhibited on mantelpieces. God is not this kind of model-boat builder. He is interested only in actual boats which sink or sail in an actual sea.

The process whereby God helps the watchman discover himself therefore involves the continued living of actual life, shocks and all, by the actual, blind self. The process, then, of moving out of darkness and into light is mostly a process of being cleansed by a God-directed experience. Forward motion is required. Risks must be run. Life as it now is must go on. This becomes a process of step-by-step enlightenment because God is now entering.

[3] Matthew 6:22.

For the clergyman in his work the shocks and risks are abundant. There is that sermon which seemed to be a failure, the encounter with the guild president who is opposed to his policies, the vestryman or deacon or elder who has controlled the congregation for a generation and who intends to keep on doing so. Then there is the clergyman's own hungry ego, his tendency to bad temper and distaste for some parts of his job. Perhaps he loves to preach but hates to call, or *vice versa*.

4   RECOVERY OF THE IMAGE

When God enters this picture, some changes immediately occur in the clergyman's mode of accepting himself. First of all, he puts less trust in his own rationalizations, be they self-excusing or self-accusing. Self-accusation is not the real cure for self-excusing, unless enough light has entered to make the self-accusation a true one. These impulses to excuse or to accuse oneself are referred by the future watchman to prayer. He restrains his temptation to analyze until the light of God makes some true analysis possible.

Another consequence of the entry of God is that the future watchman finds himself becoming a faster learner from experience. No longer is he such a prey to impulse as to repeat the same mistake, walk into the same trap, over and over again.

Still another benefit is seen in his increased ability to discover and accept unpleasant facts about himself. Now that God is his stay, and God will have nothing to do with untruth, even the unpleasant truth is now embraced, and another step is taken toward the light. Thus, humility is discovered as a happy attitude, instead of a groveling one. It turns out to be nothing other than the discovery of solid rock on which to build one's house.

By these stages self-discovery is also the acquisition of inward light and of spiritual foundations. It is more easily described than performed, because the process is at times extremely painful. Whoever can accept this confusion in himself, whoever can submit to the humiliations of his own mistakes, whoever can absorb without revenge the unfair judgments which others direct at him, this person is paying a price.

Apart from belief and prayer, the total price is too much for everyone. No one can stand repeated retreat while others seem to go ahead, nor the prospect of ultimate failure, without some compensating artifice whereby he either walls himself in or pretends that defeat is victory. The "ivory tower" of the successful and the insanity of the unsuccessful, these are the extreme ingredients of which most people's lives are a frustrated mixture. The watchman must endure the same agonies, but for him, because of God, they must be a progress toward soundness of eye.

5 NOTES OF PROPHECY

These things being so, the true watchman of the house of Israel does not go to his work because he likes it. He does it because God has moved him to it. For his own part, he is too aware of his incompetence to prophesy in the spirit merely of one who loves his work. On the other hand, neither is he sullen about it. Since it is a work of God, it is a work of love for the restoration of life.

Because he has a transcendent point of reference in God, the experienced watchman also has an answer for that horned dilemma of the clergyman, the choice between popularity and antagonism. The real source of this dilemma is the rooting of human activity in the self. If it is I myself alone who am acting, then indeed I am embarrassed by the choice between good public relations and telling the truth. Obviously I should not relate unpleasant truths about others with no purpose in mind. That goes by the name of gossip. When, however, my duties as pastor force me to make a decision, to take a stand, the matter is different. Not long ago a Roman Catholic bishop made a decision about racial integration in the worship of the churches within his diocese. At the same time and in the same part of the country, a Presbyterian minister gave forthright, rational guidance on the same problem. Both, at a cost to themselves, bore witness to the truth, and it is safe to say that their union with God was the source of their witness.

If we are watchmen of the Lord, the dilemma between popularity and antagonism has its solution. Instead of presenting itself as a dilemma, it now presents itself as a price to be paid. We have the prophetic function in Christ, not in our own right—which preserves love and humility; and not in our own strength—which saves us from sullen stoicism.

As watchmen of the Lord we have the serenity and the authority necessary for the office. In this connection he has given us an example. We read, in the fourth Gospel, "For I have not spoken on my own authority; the Father who sent me has himself given me commandment what to say and what to speak." [4] If he in his perfection referred all things to the Father, how much more need I refer to Christ all that I do as a watchman.

[4] John 12:49.

When I wait for his command, no chip is on my shoulder, no frozen rigidity results.

We must also remember the hunger of the laity. They have seen us, deceived by flattery, sell truth short. They have seen us love to lecture more than to preach. They have seen us build on the shifting sands of popularity. They have come to church for something better than that. They are heartened and renewed by the sight of a pastor who is willing to confess his limitations in order to wait for God, and to speak as God directs him to speak.

Chapter 3

᠊᠊

GUIDEPOSTS

To help make the transfer from theory to practice, there are patterns in the New Testament for the watchman to follow. Let us now review these, distinguishing, where necessary, the changeless truth from the altered idiom and equipment with which we must proclaim it today.

1 THE SACRIFICE OF SUCCESS

The most perfect of all watchmen is obviously a model to be observed and, in our limited capacities, imitated. The New Testament represents Jesus as continuing the work of the prophets. He unashamedly rests his own higher teaching on moral foundations laid by his predecessors. He also declares his "woes," his warnings, and his dooms. What are some of the characteristics of his prophecy?

First of all, he shares with all the prophets the claim to speak as an oracle of God, rather than out of his own personal reaction. He backs this up by a life of prayer made possible by frequent withdrawals from the come-and-go of society. He is saved from society before attempting to save society. This, moreover, has cost him the great sacrifice of society's kind of success. In his temptation he has had to reject an attractive opportunity to have "all the kingdoms of the world," [1] and to give his life work a starting chance he is obliged to withdraw from the religious centers of Judea, in order not to meet, abortively, the fate of John the Baptist. His home community in the North also makes light of him. His lot is cast with the multitudes who do him no political good. Far from meeting the "right" people, he lets the wrong people meet him, yet he must warn them not to follow him unless they too can pay a price.

2 THE COMMON DOCTRINE

Another characteristic of Jesus as a watchman is his use of standard, orthodox doctrine. This is a point too often obscured by the Christian anxiety to point up the new in his teaching. Whatever our motives for insisting on the uniqueness of the teaching of Jesus, we who believe in him as the Son of God can easily overdo the emphasis on newness. A candid reading of the New Testament forces the conviction that his greatest weapon in the attack upon the Pharisees was the standard scriptural teaching of the Pharisees themselves, rather than his claims to being theologically different. Perhaps his nearest approach to subversive moral doctrine was his open breaking of rules for keeping the Sabbath and his scriptural defense of these actions. It should not escape us, even here, that his defense was scriptural. One can say in real truth that Jesus, in criticizing the Pharisees, was himself a doctrinal Pharisee. He appealed to the same Scriptures.

[1] Matthew 4:8 ff.

3   THE WEAPONS OF LOGIC AND FACT

Logic and fact also were weapons of the Ideal Watchman. Modern religious fear of these weapons is an ominous symptom of our spiritual sickness. We act and talk as though logic and fact had best be kept out of our religious conversations, for fear that damage may be done. What damage? Are we, too, vulnerable to the activities of the mind? If so we must be enemies instead of friends of the Lord.

He did not attack basic doctrine, as we have seen. He rather drew different practical conclusions from this doctrine by the use of logic and fact in the act of interpretation. The Pharisees, having the right scriptural teaching about God, his care for men, man's unworthiness in relation to the holiness of God, the honor given to the ancient prophets, etc., had ceased to apply this teaching honestly and with common sense. The result was an elaborated legal system which was rationally in conflict with its own premises. In criticism of this situation, Jesus won his ground by homely logic, an appeal to common sense. For example, "Is it lawful on the sabbath to do good or to do harm, to save life or to kill?" [2] is so simple that an unspoiled child would think of it, whereas an elaborated system would negate it.

Fact, also, is introduced where logic fails. To understand human life is to know that logic by itself is often inadequate for handling the more complex problems. Psychology describes and psychiatry diagnoses those areas of personal value in which logic is appropriate only after factual truth has been introduced. Even though he lived his earthly life in the pre-scientific

[2] Mark 3:4.

era, Jesus by precept and parable introduces fact as prior to logic on many occasions. The fact of ownership supplies the logic for the generosity of the householder who overpaid the last-hired of his laborers.[3] The fact of sickness supplies the logic for the healing of the demoniacs without reproof.[4] The fact of fatherhood supplies the logic for the festivities at the prodigal son's return.[5]

Logic and fact, facets of truth, are always on the side of true religion, whereas they are embarrassing problems for false religion.

4 THE WEAPON OF EXAMPLE

In the very act of noting this we have confronted another facet of ideal prophecy, namely, the prophecy of action. Because Jesus lived as God wanted him to live, he "spoke" so loudly in deed that the community was aroused as though he had spoken in word. The very actions of the man opened him up to a professional attack. To us this means that the pulpit is not the only place for prophecy. Not only the clergy as God's spokesmen, but the laity and the clergy as God's laborers, are being watchmen in deed.

The method of personal example is not to be despised. Tension, plus prayer, plus obedience, is a formula for producing Christian character; and the Christian character has prophecy implicit in it. People of good will, who are oppressed by the distortions and false thinking which society imposes on them, are definitely guided toward the truth by the mere sight of a person who is free from the surrounding falsehood. "Let your

[3] Matthew 20:1 ff.   [4] Matthew 9:32 ff.   [5] Luke 15:22-24.

light so shine before men, that they may see your good works
and give glory to your Father who is in heaven." [6]

5 THE ETHICS OF RELATIONSHIP

With respect to content, we should be made uneasy by the
preponderant importance Jesus gives to the ethics of relationship, as contrasted with the ethics of individual propriety. The
ethics of mere individual propriety may well reflect the "good
manners" emphasis of the French salons more than it reflects
the New Testament. The great trend toward "social ethics" in
our own day may be looked upon as a groping toward the rela-
tional ethics of Jesus. In so far as social ethics aims at human
justice, it is moving in the right direction; but in so far as it
puts its hope in political arrangements only, it is extraordinar-
ily naïve. No ethics resting on community arrangement will
ever cut as deep as the demand Christ makes on the individual
under any arrangement. What he asks is not "What kind of a
social arrangement do you live under?" What he asks is: "What
do you do to your neighbor?"

6 THE ABANDONMENT OF SECURITY

The deeply personal quality of prophecy in the Bible calls
attention to another element in the prophet's way of life,
namely, his involvement in the realities of life. When we noted
that Jesus was in a sense withdrawn from society in order to
save society we were looking at a withdrawal from attitudes

[6] Matthew 5:16.

and from mental enslavement. It was not a withdrawal from experience. If anything, Jesus was more identified with the survival problems of life than other people, rather than less so. He abandoned the securities for the sake of the survival areas of life, and bade his disciples do the same. Yet this daring sacrifice was not made in order merely to seek adventure. Its avowed goal was to obtain the only ultimate security, namely that of the Kingdom of God.

Most Christians, emerging without choice into a "Christian" society, have never been in a position of deliberate and thoughtful abandonment of the world's securities. We would be abnormal if we sought such a sacrifice merely for its own sake. Yet there are a few to whom God has thus directly spoken. A far greater number of us face imposed insecurities unwillingly. Every time the rug is thus pulled out from under us we are forced into the revealing encounter with brutal fact. It is revealing because the disaster tests whether our "house" was designed by the master architect who builds his houses upon the rock, or whether we have built ours foolishly upon sand.[7]

7 THE USE OF BOOKS

This involvement in the security area of life and its consequent revelation are the *sine qua non* of experience for the Christian watchman. If he has had this in some degree, then and only then will he also receive some real benefit from books on the subject. The book can perform a useful function in that it sometimes extends the reader's imaginative experience, or adds to his stock of useful information and constructive com-

[7] Matthew 7:24 ff.

munication. However, in this age of quantity publication the good offices of the book are abused like all other good offices. The most frequent abuse is the tendency to read merely in order "to keep up." Keep up with what? Other people? The truth? In our gregarious hunger to keep up with other people we are merely aping the multitudes whom Jesus likened to sheep not having a shepherd. If we think we are hungering for truth, we must be deluding ourselves. Real, live truth is a powerful medicine, which most of us can stand only in measured doses.

The true watchman knows this. He will use a book in its place, but his real concern is in the foundations of his own house.

8   OBSERVATION BY SHARING AND SELF-CONTROL

In the degree to which he has done this and has achieved some relative self-knowledge, however slight, the watchman has his eyes opened also to the world around him. His observation of other people may now really begin, now that he knows something of his own blindness and his own need for charity. To use the metaphor of baseball, the true watchman is neither a grandstand manager nor umpire. He is playing the game himself. Jesus did not have a grandstand seat, nor should his follower.

There is, however, the important difference that the followers, unlike their Lord, are confused sinners. Just because they are also involved in the heat of the action they must resist their own temptations first before they can see what is going on with a clear eye. Let our motto be: "Resist first, observe afterward, and speak last."

9 THE PURPOSE

This leads up to the fundamental requirement of a right purpose. It is so easy to acquire a wrong one! We do not observe the sins of society in order to see how stupid people are, and to enjoy our own fancied superiority. Our purpose as watchmen is derived from the vision of the glorious possibilities of human nature as God made it. Saint Paul speaks of "the glorious liberty of the children of God." [8] From our standpoint as Christians we may speak of the glorious vision of the children of God. God has made human nature to be glorious. As we observe the evils which destroy this possibility, our reaction is one of sorrow. The vehemence of prophecy is to destroy the destroyer; to give human nature a chance to come into its own, in God. It is, therefore, a vehemence of love.

10 THE APPROACH TO OTHERS

If we really have a true purpose, we shall more likely have a true approach to others, which means that we shall avoid being watch*dogs*. There is a certain temperament which takes to the watchdog idea too readily. Let us consider it this way. It is not a Protestant monopoly, but a Catholic doctrine also, found in Saint Thomas Aquinas,[9] that only God can convert the soul. This makes the difference between proselyting and converting.

[8] Romans 8:21.　　　[9] *Summa Theologica* I, Qu. cvi, art. II.

Man, misusing his influence, and taking a sectarian position, proselytes. God converts. The Christian's function is that of a messenger, a watchman, and a steward of the mysteries. Furthermore, God has so fashioned human nature that even he cannot convert without the co-operation of the person to be converted.

So, we are not wardens of other souls as though keepers of a prison. We are watchmen to free souls who have within themselves the responsibilities of choice. It is not a matter of fussing over people, or of trying to manage their lives for them. It is, rather, a matter of helping people clear away the barriers which separate them from Christ. Just as much self-effacement is required in this as in any other personal relationship among free agents. Self-effacement does not empty prophecy of authority. It fills it with the authority of Christ, which no one can gainsay.

11 NEW TESTAMENT METHOD AND IDIOM IN THE LIGHT OF TODAY

There are ways in which the Gospels are a help in our search for an effective method, but there are other factors involved requiring us to translate both the method of Christ and the situation into a different idiom. Jesus used the traditional communication of his day: the current rabbinical mode of teaching in short, crisply worded precepts and parables, easily listened to, and designed to be easily remembered. Furthermore, this method was adapted for use in public places, so that the audience was selected by free motivation rather than by sectarian affiliation. A reasonable cross section of the population was reached.

Today our clergy are limited by the church-sermon tradition. Nothing can nor should be done to eliminate this, but we need to recognize its limitations. By the sermon tradition the clergyman is obliged to develop ideas rather than to pinpoint them. The developed idea courts the theoretical and argumentative rather than the applicable and decisive, nor is it so easily remembered. Also, now that we are spoiled by the invention of printing, the receiver's mind is less trained to retentive listening.

What is more, the sermon audience is selected rather by sectarian affiliation than by natural motivation. The preacher is not really facing a cross section of the population. The listeners are people who have at least come to church on that occasion. Most of them are, presumably, baptized Christians. They have made some kind of start, and are expecting to be guided still further along the road. Therefore, if we must transfer New Testament methods to our present work, let us remember that the Epistles represent our situation more than do the Gospels. Hence, the preaching side of the clergyman's function as a watchman has that same leaning toward warning and renewal that we find in the Epistles.

Occasionally someone attempts to transcend this limitation and to reach, as we say, "the unchurched." Street preaching is so removed from our common experience that only the rarely gifted can hope to do it with constructive effect. More often a church will attempt by diverting methods and unconventional advertising to be, itself, a sort of crossroads meetinghouse. Here the constructive effect seems to depend on the clarity with which the true goal is held in view. Is it to be great success, or evangelizing? The two are not the same.

12   THE CHANGED ENVIRONMENT

Whatever the method employed, the environmental situation also has its similarities to and differences from that of the New Testament. Most of us suffer from a temptation to apply uncritically the Bible idiom to the situations of our own day. The terms "Pharisee" and "hypocrite," for example, are thrown out loosely, without enough care about whether they are being applied in the appropriate places. A little thought about the things which are similar and the things which are different will help avoid this pitfall.

Basic human nature is the same now as then. We still seek the glory which comes from one another, instead of the glory which comes from God.[10] We still honor the Prophets, while ignoring the truths which the Prophets proclaimed.[11] We still violate a good doctrine by the neglect of logic and fact. In other words, man's enslavement to the world and his slowness in self-criticism is universal and perpetual. Yet, on the differences side of the ledger, we must note that Israel was a theocracy which had lost political freedom; ours is a politically free country which is only feebly theocratic. Broadly stated, the American still says "God, I thank thee that I am not like other men," [12] but he places his pride in the acquisition of other than religious merits.

As the watchman encounters the situations in the Church and in the world which test his watchmanship, he grows more and more to treasure the solid foundation of religious truth. To

[10] John 5:44.   [11] Matthew 23:29–31.   [12] Luke 18:11.

use the equipment available, and to acquire that rocklike base provided by Christ costs him a price in the sacrifice of self which no man has paid perfectly. The happy corollary, on the other hand, is that in so far as he does come equipped he is in as much possession of unshakable truth as the successful engineer. His joy does not come from illusory pride, but from the ability to apply a knowledge which the crumbling world sorely needs.

We are passing out of that time when religion could be looked upon as the decorative touch upon a social structure which put its real faith in the control of matter. It is now evident that both the decorative religion and the social structure have been misunderstood. The social structure is seen needing another kind of assured knowledge to accompany its control of matter. The religion, on the other hand, turns out not to be a decorative, dispensable ornament, but the foundation of the structure.

Chapter 4

THEOLOGICAL LEADERSHIP

After examining himself, developing his communion with God, and gleaning materials and methods from the Bible, the watchman cannot neglect contemporary Christian leadership. In so far as the governing body of the watchman's own allegiance offers guidance in current moral problems, this guidance is made available to him directly; but in so far as it has come from high and independent theological sources he is under the burden of seeking it out and interpreting it for himself. It is the aim of this chapter to help this search and interpretation by an outline of the principal changes in theological leadership since the turn of the century and the background out of which they sprang.

It is sometimes important to stand at a distance from a moving scene in order capture its major trends. When we do this for the first two decades of the century, there is evident a rising emphasis on the social gospel and a declining emphasis on doctrine.

The movement of the social gospel had as its major theme the building of God's kingdom in contemporary society by direct action on the part of Christians. This called for a greater Christian participation in democratic politics, more generous philanthropic activity on behalf of the underprivileged, and, as a natural corollary, more vigorous agitation for the correction of social wrongs. The movement had been gathering momentum at the close of the nineteenth century, but it enjoyed its most forceful expression in the personality and writing of Walter Rauschenbusch. His book, *Christianity and the Social Crisis,* which appeared in 1907, made a prophetic impact. He followed this up by many other works on the subject until his death in 1918.

Still standing at a distance, however, we can see that doctrinally the direction of Christian thought was negative throughout this period, rather than positive. The dominant problem with doctrine was its unsound position in the face of the growing impact of scientific achievement. With the advantage of hindsight we can understand that the theologians of the time would at first lose their way in the attempt to relate the faith of the non-scientific Bible to the thinking of an increasingly scientific age. A few defenders of orthodoxy braced themselves to maintain dogmatic tradition, and thereby were trapped into being looked upon as behind the times.

More numerous were those who hastened to welcome the discoveries of the human mind and proceeded to resolve the conflict between these discoveries and their beliefs by converting the latter, subtly, into abstract ideals.

This weakening of belief reacted on the movement of the social gospel both favorably and unfavorably. Favorably, it won support for the idea of the social gospel as the essence of Christianity and thus gained for it a following which otherwise it would not have had. Those who could not believe in miracles could retain their status as Christians by making Christianity identical with the social gospel.

On the other hand, when the time came for thoughtful people of the Church to take a more positive stance as believers, the shallowness of this identification brought the name "social gospel" into disrepute. After the death of Rauschenbusch, the movement which he had so gloriously led bore its best fruit in conjunction with a return to faith, rather than as a movement in some ways divorced from faith.

What caused this return to faith? No one can discern the inward motions of the Spirit except by their fruits, yet the change in the outward situation was before everyone's eyes, a change so radical that the theological climate could not remain unaffected by it.

World War I must still be reckoned as a major reversal for human ideals in the West. We mid-century citizens have seen such far greater horrors in World War II, and in the development of atomic weapons, that we need to be reminded that the shock to human ideals provided by a war is not only in proportion to the degree of destruction of that war, but is also in proportion to the naïveté of the ideals destroyed. While World War I was relatively less devastating than war today, it was not less but more of a moral shock.

Prior to the year 1914 a majority of Americans were ready to believe that war had finally succumbed to the advance of civilization. True, there recently had occurred the Spanish-American War and the Russo-Japanese War, but these were considered anachronisms, not likely to happen again. In this naïve climate of opinion miracles were unnecessary, as well as hard to believe in, and God could readily become the sum of human ideals. Against that background, for the leading nations of the civilized world to engage in a more extensive war than had ever been known was an event catastrophic to the abstract faith of the idealists. It is true that the victorious Allies pretended, as nations, to be their old selves once again after the war, but no such pretense was possible in ruined Germany, nor in the minds of the perceptive anywhere.

The two most characteristic reactions of theology were a recovery of the sense of revelation as something given to man from the outside, and a recovery of the doctrine of original sin. When Karl Barth published his commentary on the Epistle to the Romans in 1919, he began the process whereby the Bible's doctrine of a transcendent God was restored to full rank in Protestant theology. No longer can it be supposed that man, in a sense, discovers God by searching for him. According to the Bible, it is the creator God who declares himself to man in a manner far transcending man's capacity for rational search.

The doctrine of original sin was made to live again, not through some obscurantist defender of tradition, but through the vital, critical personality of Reinhold Niebuhr, whose pastoral experiences among the automobile workers of Detroit quickened his perception of the ambiguous position of the Church in society. On the one hand the Church is holy because God is holy. On the other hand she actually maintains herself by participation in the inescapable sins of the community. He developed the Biblical view of the fallen nature of man in conflict with the demand of a holy God for socially responsible living, and showed the impossibility of facing that demand without encountering also the opposing sin embedded in our natures, both socially and individually. His writings have been numerous, but his book, *Moral Man and Immoral Society,* published in 1932, made the initial impact.

There have followed, of course, other trends of theological leadership. The rediscovery of the writings of Kierkegaard through their translation into English reinforced the notions of encounter and decision in man's relations with God, and blended with a certain cluster of philosophical insights popularized as "existentialism." Rudolph Bultmann returns to the problems raised for belief by the existentialist approach and by the unverifiable nature of the New Testament accounts; while Paul Tillich provides a magnificent synthesis of ontology and Biblical faith. The so-called Fundamentalists, for their part, have shown that their positions are not so obscurantist as their accusers would have had us believe.

For the watchman, however, the principal significance of these later movements is their witness to the growing interest in theology among people generally. A generation ago the grand yet difficult constructions of Dr. Tillich could not have had the following they enjoy today. Theology, formerly despised, is now revived in the public esteem. This must mean something, however unmeasurable, in terms of a searching after things religious.

What is most significant in recent theological trends, what we ought to keep our sights trained on, are the movements characterized by Karl Barth and Reinhold Niebuhr. The recovery of the God who reveals himself, and of the doctrine of original sin, goes deeper into the watchman's task than any other theological trend of our day. This recovery means that we have, once again, a union of Christian ethics with Christian belief. It is the holy God who calls his people to do justly. When society fails to exhibit this behavior, it is not God who falls, but society. No mere faith in abstract ideals can stand up straight in this contemporary world, where vast destruction seems so much easier than the building of a harmonious society.

The Church at large has responded to this theological leadership by taking stands on social issues. In the case of some religious bodies, responsible public decisions have shown a surprising reversal in the direction of a readiness to criticize the social tradition. An example of this is afforded by the Episcopal Church which, during World War I, removed the Bishop of Utah from his jurisdiction because of his pacifist statements, but which, in 1955, transferred its triennial convention to Honolulu rather than participate in non-integrated arrangements in Houston, Texas. Similar examples of an independent stance in moral questions have been supplied by other religious bodies.

This, to the watchman, has a twofold significance. It shows him, first of all, that the Church as an ecclesiastical body is now aware that to be a Christian means something more than to be a standard citizen. The Church used to form its policies on the supposition that Christianity and standard citizenship were very nearly synonymous terms. Now all this is changed. Standard citizenship is seen not necessarily to involve being a Christian, and to be a Christian is seen to involve being something much more than a standard citizen. The Church has at last awakened to her greater message and her greater resource. Even in her quiet moments she is beginning to behave like the leaven which leavens the lump.

Second, this means to the individual watchman that he is not alone. The body of which he is a member is beginning to speak with him. To be sure, as a Christian community we have far to go before we can say that the common witness is always forceful and timely. Yet a great change for the better has taken place. At least some corporate leadership is available to guide and encourage the local clergy in their role as watchmen.

PART TWO

<<<<<<<<<<<<<<<<<<<<<<<<<<<<<<<<<<<<<<<<<<<<<<<<<<

The Environment

Chapter 5

TURBULENT SKIES

When the watchman looks at his world he finds it so complex and dynamic that he might well despair of being able to make any useful observation about it. The people of one community may behave toward social issues quite differently from the people of another community. Even within one city, a local transit strike or a startling item of world news may find opinion lined up according to cultural levels, or economic levels, or religious affiliation, in such a way as to rule out simple conclusions. More baffling still, the same affiliations in the same community may change direction from decade to decade on the same issues.

Yet, if this spiritual environment is complex and shifting, it nevertheless has some discernible characteristics which can and should be noted. The watchman is, in this respect, like the weatherman: he would be derelict in his duty if he did not state the broadly obvious. Among these discernible characteristics of our spiritual weather chart there are two which must ever be kept in mind throughout our observations. First, the spiritual climate, like the natural climate, is dominated by mass movement in which the individual is usually submerged and swept along. Second, the observer is dealing with material which is partly predictable and partly unpredictable.

1 THE GROUP AND THE INDIVIDUAL

Our tradition of liberty tends to blind us to the submerging of the individual. Dwellers in the western democracies, and the more western the more this is true, are sold their ideologies on the supposition of intellectual freedom. It is a commonplace that we are proud of our right to choose freely. An ideology, therefore, simply avoids mentioning situations which curtail choice. So successful is this polarized approach in the distribution of ideas in the West that only the cynics and psychiatrists are left to reveal the compulsive thinking which really underlies our mental habits.

We see this quite easily in our predecessors. With no trouble at all we accept the fact that the idealism prevailing before the first world war was a group phenomenon, in which the well-meaning individual played a blindly passive role. The metaphor of a herd of sheep is one which we mid-century sophisticates think very appropriate to the era of McKinley, Theodore Roosevelt, and William Howard Taft. So it has always been. Each age of human history feels comfortably superior to the age immediately preceding its own. The legend of "the golden age" must be put far enough back to serve as a mere companion to an equally legendary Utopia of the future. In nonlegendary history we are always superior.

The blindness of this attitude is an ever-disastrous fact. We are a herd of sheep now, no less passively following without a real leader. The mere change of direction has not altered this incapacity to see and to think independently. The rush to grasp and devour the latest pessimism is no more a free-choice act than was the comfortable enjoyment of mass idealism a generation ago. We, like our forebears, must belong. We, too, are children of environment.

This is not to deny that real freedom exists. It is only to say that much which passes for freedom is mere gregariousness and, therefore, a source of delusion. Substantial freedom is inseparable from substantial truth. It comes at the price of the encounter with fact which mere gregariousness cannot pay. The truly free exhibit characteristics which show that they have done something more than merely belong to the group. If they are in positions of leadership they have things to say which the group either does not know or is unwilling to admit. If they are in subordinate positions their contribution is in some way uncommon. These observations are true of the wicked as well as the good. Hitler, for example, owed some of the ingredients of his power to his imprisonment. The saints owe some of their qualities to withdrawal, whether voluntary or involuntary.

That is not to say that the path to freedom is antisocial. On the contrary, truly free people are the most social, but they have paid a price for their freedom which the group could not pay for them, and which they agonized over in some way apart from the group. The deceptive nature of our situation arises from mankind's perennial habit of counterfeiting its true leaders instead of imitating them. The true is always, in some way, the solitary, and the group action is always, in some way, untrue.

2 THE PREDICTABLE AND THE UNPREDICTABLE

With regard to the unpredictable quality of winds of doctrine, the observation imposes itself upon us that sociological movements are far too complex and interactive for the victims of them to forecast detailed consequences. Massively, and in the large, we can and should predict. The stream can be seen inevitably to be destined for the river, and the river for the ocean; but that helpless leaf! It may surprise you and lodge against a twig. The coming of summer is a certainty in springtime, but whether those buds will be nipped by a late frost, that is unpredictable.

The events of our own day are sweeping us along in an unmistakable direction, but they and their individual effects are as mixed and unpredictable as the air currents in a turbulent atmosphere. In the religious concern, no less than in other cultural concerns, a given individual, congregation, or community may be tossed almost any way and anywhere. One and the same person may belong to the *avant-garde* in his conscious expressions while being conservative in his practical relationships. For this reason it is foolish to ignore fashions of thought which are on the decrease, and which were at their height a generation ago. The situation in every age is so confused that the ideologies of the past may continue to carry a majority with them even though they have ceased to be the mode. Conversely, the ideologies which enjoy the reputation of liberating the daring from old enslavement may be just as enslaving because they have become the mode. We all pass more easily from slavery to slavery than from slavery to freedom.

Expressing this in terms of the analogy of democratic elections, we can say that salvation is guaranteed neither by the majority nor by the minority. It is neither a vote for the new nor for the old, but rather for whatever is discovered to be true. "Every scribe who has been trained for the kingdom of heaven is like a householder who brings out of his treasure what is new and what is old." [1]

Nevertheless, when we try to assess the spiritual environment in which we live, it is helpful to take notice of characteristic order, sources, and directions, just as a meteorologist notes conflicting wind directions and pressure changes. It does make some difference to us whether a given influence is a survival from the past or a new and developing trend, and if the latter, whether it is likely to gather force or die.

3 WINDS OF DOCTRINE

Turning now more specifically to the present spiritual situation in the United States, it is possible to list the more obvious surviving attitudes which cannot be discounted even though they appear doomed. No one can claim that prewar *optimism* has really been abandoned. The very gaiety with which we despise all uncomfortable disciplines as hindrances to the rich life reveals an optimism which refuses to surrender to the gloomy facts. With this goes the cult of the strong individual who is proud to consider himself the epitome of all that is best

[1] Matthew 13:52.

in *humanism*. This, in turn, still leads to the *negativism* of the childish within us, which finds something wrong with the new ideas unless they be our own. In a rich country like ours it is inevitable that *materialism* abound in innumerable individuals, who might reject the word in principle but who have made physical comfort a self-satisfying way of life. Students from Christian homes still go religiously unprepared into the *academic* life. The habit of *dissent* still outruns its original purpose and prevents the development of the total Christian life. All these ensnare the Church in the error of never saying anything unpleasant or unpopular; and this results in the ultimate in religious degradation, the *loss of the sense of the holy*.

Optimism, individualistic humanism, negativism, materialism, the weakening of belief, the habit of dissent, and the loss of the sense of the holy—these are some of the influential survivals from the earlier decades of our century. More recently a growing cynicism, of a healthy sort, has been acting to cancel these survivals and to replace them with new positives in the common life.

As these movements converge and conflict in the stream of human reaction, they deserve a closer study. Each of them has an anatomy and a set of relationships of some importance to the person who is religiously concerned. We cannot hope to be exact in the midst of such motion and complexity. We can only catch the obvious and the salient. Detachment is not the lot of any of us, but neither have we the right to run uncritically with the crowd. If our involvement has been with prayer and our confusion acknowledged, we should be beneficiaries of that normal eyesight which is granted to the humble.

Chapter 6

THE SURVIVING ATTITUDES

Attitudes, traits of mind, ideologies, and popular philosophies do not spring up full-blown overnight. Nor do they die abrupt and complete deaths. The watchman is helped in his task if he understands that the Christian view is surrounded with hardy perennials of earlier eras as well as recent hybrids, and can put his finger on their weaknesses.

Among these traits and attitudes are optimism, humanism, negativism, materialism, the academic outlook, dissent, and the loss of the sense of holiness. Because it is the classic American trait, let us set forth optimism first, then view the others in turn.

1 OPTIMISM

Optimism is the trait which is found *par excellence* among Americans. It is that view of life which is confident that "day by day in every way, things are getting better and better." It is not, let us admit, unconnected with endeavor and hard work. Of all the ideologies we are to consider, it is the oldest and most native to this country. Since the conditions which produced American optimism are changing and passing away, it is possible that optimism itself may be a thing of the past in about three generations, but as a philosophy of life it is still very powerful among us. The depression and the second world war did not destroy it.

The colonizing of America was selective, in a very obvious way, with regard to the types of personalities it attracted: the business adventurers, the religious and political dissenters, the romancers, etc. A person had to have a deep-seated reason for setting out on so chancy a venture as the New World represented, and many of these reasons continued to motivate immigrants throughout the history of the nation's independence. The forebears of most of us were indeed an enterprising lot.

Enterprise by itself would not produce optimism, but the prodigal resources of an undeveloped continent have given us a history which would produce optimism in a saint. Not only has there been an abundance of land, and an ever movable frontier, but this raw abundance happened to coincide with an industrial revolution throughout the western world, so that the means of exploitation increased in geometric proportions over a period of 150 years, while the resources to be exploited were still beyond the imagination.

Any American community with a stationary population was an oddity. Normal cities and towns were accommodating more people year by year. Parallel to increasing population was a rising standard of living. What this has resulted in from the standpoint of making money is too obvious. There have been wars, panics, and fiascoes of other kinds, but never such as to put a permanent stop to mounting prosperity.

From the standpoint of character, this has meant that almost anyone who showed a minimum of diligence and reliability could earn a decent living. Elaborate training was seldom necessary, even for special types of work. Myriads of self-made men rose to success like steam in a boiling kettle. The log-cabin tradition served as a symbol of two ideals, human equality and the well-tested life.

With this process going on for five generations, it is no wonder that we Americans became optimists. Nature, and the national experience with nature, have made us so. It is hard, therefore, for us to understand our European neighbors, for whom nature is not prodigal in proportion to the population, and prosperity as we know it is the privilege of the few. By the same token it is hard for Europeans to understand us.

We are now in a period when the causes of optimism are being taken away. During the thirties we saw financial values shrink over a long period of time, in a manner having little relation to the temporary panics of the past. The very word "panic" was inapplicable to the depression, which was too persistent a fact to be called a panic. It no longer seemed odd for the population of a town to remain stationary, or for willing, diligent, and trained people to be out of work. Nevertheless, the optimism generated by a century and a half of rapid material progress will outlive its causes for a while.

Since this optimism is an American trait, we Americans naturally think it a virtue. Why not? What is wrong with it?

The answer is that life is not always like that. Seldom is nature able to be so prodigal, just when man is learning new tricks of material exploitation and development. Societies and individuals alike seldom can expect to have such an easy time of it. Optimism, then, is a mistaken view of life, and because it is mistaken, it is wrong.

From the spiritual standpoint, the habit of optimism takes most of the depth out of religious experience and makes it a shallow thing indeed. It is easy to believe that God is in his heaven when all's right with the world, and there doesn't seem to be a necessity for seeking any closer relationship with God than that. Under lush circumstances the virtue of hope loses its meaning. Why does the optimist need hope, when things are at their best already, as far as he is concerned; or if not at their best, at least on the way to becoming so?

The theory of progressive evolution fits into the optimist's scheme of things nicely, because evolution is simply the cosmic way of achieving the best by gradual stages. There is nothing in the scientific theory of evolution which is contrary to the Christian faith; but the optimist's interpretation of evolution is contrary both to science and the faith. Science and the faith agree that the world is not everlasting, at least from the standpoint of its being a place of habitation for man. This idea is a great shock to the evolutionary optimist, or in fact to any kind of optimist.

Now it may be true that the academic theory of progressive evolution is out of date, and scientifically informed people no longer hold to it, but as an un-thought-out, practical outlook upon life, it has had a broad grip on the population. It makes us, as a people, ill-prepared for future contingencies, less inclined than we should be to turn to the Holy Spirit for guidance and to cultivate the virtues of faith and hope. To most people in this country, the New Testament example of the lilies of the field is a beautiful bit of poetic and romantic prose, but it has little practical force as long as a man can do well by himself and there is plenty to do it with.

We have all had contact with American families who have been faced with the struggle for existence at its hardest. Some of them have developed a splendid faith, through which God has helped them. But we are here looking at the national character and experience in the large, in so far as it generates a wide-spread outlook on life.

In the individual, this optimism imposed by society accounts for a good deal of what we call complacency. Complacent people are not always hardened in pride. Sometimes they are just blind to the future; unaware of large areas of life, and therefore unprepared for life. A watchman's word of warning will often be well received. Disaster, too, is an eye-opener in those with some religious faith with which to meet it. In at least a proportion of the families that have faced disaster there has come the increased knowledge of God and of his readiness to hear the appeal of the stricken.

Turning to our scriptural source, do we not learn in the New Testament that those who received the good news of the Gospel were those who were most aware of their need for it?—the poor, the maimed, the halt, the blind, the sinners; also those in good health who were bearing heavy responsibilities in life and who knew, for one reason or another, that they were not adequate for their burdens. Those who received the Gospel were not the optimists of their time, but those who had had a sobering experience with life, perhaps desperate experiences.

American optimism, then, is a natural result of the national experience, and as Americans we have probably succumbed to it more or less. Its widespread acceptance should not deceive us into thinking that it is a friend of Christianity. It allows prosperity to blind it to responsibility and danger. It has its own religion. It believes in God, but does not consider that it needs God's grace. In some respects it is closely related to materialism, which we shall consider later.

2   HUMANISM AND NEGATIVISM

Humanism is an ideology which, even in this country, has had an intellectual and a literary origin, definitely thought out and openly propagated. Its modern history is so deep that it has penetrated the thinking of the non-literary and the non-academic public.

The practical tenets of humanism may be stated, briefly, as follows: Man is the highest knowable being. There may be something higher than man, but if there is a being higher than man, that being is not knowable. Hence, there is no genuine basis for religion except man's own religion of himself.

This much is held by non-theistic humanism. There is also a theistic humanism, quite willing to adopt a mild religion, but still believing that man can, essentially, save himself.

It is therefore through culture and a well-ordering of himself in civilization that man makes good his highest potentialities. He has within himself the power to do this. The only alternative is complete pessimism.

An outstanding American exponent of humanism was Irving Babbitt, who began his own definition in the following words:

As is well known, the word humanist was applied, first in the Italy of the fifteenth century, and later in other European countries, to the type of scholar who was not only proficient in Greek and Latin, but who at the same time inclined to prefer the humanity of the great classical writers to what seemed to him the excess of divinity in the mediaevals. This contrast between humanity and divinity was often conceived very superficially. However, the best

*of the humanists were not content with opposing a some-
what external imitation of the Ciceronian or Virgilian
elegance to the scholastic carelessness of form. They actually caught a glimpse of the fine proportionateness of
the ancients at their best. They were thus encouraged to
aim at a harmonious development of their faculties in this
world rather than at an other-worldly felicity. Each fac-
ulty, they held, should be cultivated in due measure without one-sidedness or over-emphasis, whether that of the
ascetic or that of the specialist. "Nothing too much" is indeed the central maxim of all genuine humanists, ancient
and modern.*[1]

"Nothing too much," poise, decorum, balance, self-achieved
through the study of the "humanities"—these are the watch-
words of humanism.

Humanism so defined is avowed only by a relatively small
number of literary and intellectual leaders. But out of this humanistic theory has come a practice, a course of conduct, which
has permeated the whole population. Most people are quite
able to be Christian in theory and humanist in practice, because
most people do not analyze their own philosophies of life. They
take their theory as they find it and their practice as they find
it, without bothering to reconcile the two. The majority of
Americans find their theory in church and their practice in a
secular society impregnated with humanism.

Now humanism is not wholly bad. It does not teach un-
modified selfishness and egotism. "Man" in the humanist sense
means mankind, society. The individual reaches his highest
and best when he co-operates with his fellows as a social being.

[1] "Humanism: An Essay at Definition," in *Humanism and America,* Nor-
man Foerster, ed., p. 26. Rinehart & Company, Inc., 1930.

Moreover, humanism believes in the arts and sciences and in all the finest human capacities. Its purpose is good.

What, then, is wrong with it? Why does it do harm?

First of all, it is wrong because it is inadequate. Humanism, under different names, has been tried by some of the greatest souls who ever lived, and its success has been limited to those who were lucky: the fortunate one per cent.

The Greek philosophies, the Greek arts, sculpture and oratory, were developed in a society based upon slave labor. In the Middle Ages the humanistic arts and the religious arts existed side by side for a time. Both depended upon the patronage of the wealthy. In modern times the cultivated few can afford to be humanists. Where does that leave mankind as a whole?

Life is bigger than man. It is bigger, even, than human society. If it were not so, man in society would have found the answer to life long ago.

In the second place, humanism does harm because it teaches man to have a confidence in himself which is unfounded. It makes a man blind to his own blindness; unaware of his own inadequacies. It deceives him into following a mirage; the mirage of his own, unaided self-betterment. It is a religion without sin.

When we look in the New Testament for those characters who really found life, we discover that they were people who had been made aware of their need for outside help, physically or spiritually: the blind man—"Master, let me receive my sight"; [2] the disciples, who knew that they did not have the answer to life within themselves, but who followed John the Baptist for his moral integrity, then Jesus for his unfolding word of truth. These people were not humanists.

[2] Mark 10:51.

Yet humanism, since it is in the world, has always worked its way into the Church. We read in the Revelation of Saint John the Divine (3:17), concerning the church of the Laodiceans, "You say, I am rich, I have prospered, and I need nothing; not knowing that you are wretched, pitiable, poor, blind and naked."

Man's confidence in himself keeps him from turning to God. This is the practical side of humanism; the humanism of the man in the pew who has never read Irving Babbitt.

What to do about it; how to combat it? We do not help matters by preaching against it. A sermon on humanism, if it were well presented, might be as interesting as a lecture on botany; but it would not be likely to cause a change of heart in the listener.

We need, rather, to teach people to know God, not just to know about God. Let them see that theoretical Christianity is "out," that it is just an empty shell. Christianity relates to life, not to theory. "Ask, and it will be given you; seek and you will find; knock, and it will be opened to you." [3] God *is* knowable. By this declaration the basis for humanism is removed, without our even mentioning the word.

At its worst, humanism shows itself as self-satisfied pride, lacking in common sense and in any real ability to make intelligent decisions. At its best, it is seen as a genial self-confidence, capable of a certain attainment in life because favored by nature, but not with much ability to go on when nature ceases to smile. Our function is to know God, and to make him known.

Under the term "humanism," we may include a variety of outlooks which have in common a belief in life, and a good purpose toward life, but which, for one reason or another, leave

[3] Matthew 7:7.

God out in practice and sometimes also in theory. They do their harm by being inadequate and by being misleading. Humanism permeates our common life because it does have the appeal of a good purpose, and because it is willing to ally itself with a belief in God, provided the latter remains theoretical.

There is abroad today another set of thoughts about life which does not have a good purpose. Its appeal lies in the fact that it is attractive to the lower elements of human nature, at the expense of the higher. It seems, for the time being, to buy life more cheaply; but it does this by destroying life itself.

We call this tendency "negativism" at the risk of confusion with certain abstract theories. In western theology and philosophy there has been a school of theoretical negativism which refused to ascribe positive attributes to God. Less theoretical have been the ascetic attitudes of the Greek disciplines with respect to bodily impulses, and the negative attitude of Buddhism toward desire. Our American negativism is less rational. In fact, it may actually be connected with a breakdown of the rational approach to life among the majority of people for whom humanism has been an unworkable luxury.

Negativism cannot be defined in positive terms, as can humanism, because it is a negation of life. It never congeals into a definite philosophy until it has won much territory by infiltration. Wisps, strands, and blocks of negativism find their way into society without, at first, identifying themselves. Nevertheless, without God, all civilizations settle into negativism in their old age. Our western civilization, though partly godless, is still more or less positive because it is still young.

We must not confuse negativism with cynicism. The cynic believes in life. Otherwise he would not be cynical about it.

The negativist has nothing to be cynical about. Diogenes at least set out to look for an honest man. The negativist isn't interested in finding an honest man. He considers that life is not worth bothering about beyond its necessities.

The Gospel, on the contrary, is given to those who care; to those who desire. "Blessed are those who hunger and thirst for righteousness, for they shall be satisfied." [4] This desire for life is a God-given desire. Therefore, negativism, which avoids all such desire, is openly contrary to God.

It is true that, given sufficient handicaps and sufficiently prolonged and brutal suffering, people of good will can have their normal desire blunted and damaged. To these people Christ says: "Come to me, all who labor and are heavy-laden, and I will give you rest. Take my yoke upon you, and learn from me; for I am gentle and lowly in heart, and you will find rest for your souls." [5] But the negativist is no such person. He has not ceased to desire life because of suffering. He has ceased to desire life because he is determined to keep all suffering at a distance from himself.

Negativism has many symptoms, which vary from person to person and from place to place. In one place it will show itself in a bitter antagonism to all alien groups, a ready embracing of racial and class hatreds; in another place, the predominant symptom will be an anti-intellectualism. The use of the mind is hard work, and it often hurts to think. In another place it will take the form of a flouting of all standards of conduct, presumably because everything tried has run its course to a useless end, as in "the beat generation." Negativism's more widespread and less extreme form is simply the absence of a sense of responsibility toward one's normal obligations in life. In this form it

[4] Matthew 5:6.　　　　　[5] Matthew 11:28, 29.

makes promises easily because there is no necessity for fulfilling them.

All is covered up by a glowing sentimentality. Just as cheap commercial products use sentimentality in their advertising to conceal their poor quality, so negativism finds sentimentality a convenient cover under which to operate, especially in religious circles. This fact forces us to have a look at sentimentality itself.

The trouble with sentimentality is not that it is sentimental. The sentiments are part of the God-given glory of human nature. The trouble with sentimentality is that it divorces the sentiments from the intellect and thereby distintegrates character. The Christian ideal is expressed by the Psalmist when he says: "Mercy and truth are met together; righteousness and peace have kissed each other." [6] We find this perfect meeting together of the sentiments and the intellect in Christ. The sentimentality of the present age is not a meeting together of the sentiments and the intellect at all. It is a hypocritical cloak for a selfish negativism.

The clergyman, as watchman, must learn to pierce beyond this smoke screen and see the destructive forces which lie behind it. Under the guidance of God the Holy Spirit, he must introduce a prophetic note into his preaching and teaching which will carry a counterattack into the enemy's camp. It is a pity that so many of the clergy have been deceived by the sentimentality of modern community life to such an extent as to leave prophecy almost wholly out of their preaching. Many will reject the prophet, of course, but there will always be some sincere souls who do desire the better thing, and who will be glad for the guidance.

In preaching against negativism, let us be careful not to use

[6] Psalms 85:10 (AV).

the word itself without being able to say what we mean by it. The terms of practical living into which it is translated will vary with the symptoms in each community.

Another error to avoid is that of thinking that activism is the opposite of negativism. There is already too much activism abroad, and it is not a cure for negativism. Mere activity is only a part of life, and it is only valid in so far as God directs it; God who directs activity according to his own will and who measures it according to the capacity of each individual soul.

Where humanism makes the mistake of trying to have life without having God, negativism, in its pious form, tries to have God without having life. Soon, it inevitably comes to the point of not wanting God either. People in the pews are negativists without knowing it, unable to help themselves because they are the unwitting victims of a negativist society. Yet God can help them; and we, in God, must help them to desire something better. Given the desire, and the taking of that desire to God, the victory is won.

Under the terms "humanism" and "negativism" we have included soul-killing traits which are not peculiar to these times, but are as old as human nature itself. Humanism and negativism were enemies of Christ in New Testament times, expressing themselves in the idiom of that time as they do today in current terms already examined. With a great deal of prayer and a little imagination, we should be able to read the New Testament both as an historical document and as an eternal document.

Sentimentalists have tried to rob the New Testament of its basis in concrete situations. On the other hand, those who emphasize the tangible nature of the New Testament are in danger of losing its eternal values through a failure to see that the enemy now wears different clothes and speaks a different language; but he is the same enemy. Here the problem is of translation from one idiom to another.

The humanist of Christ's day was found in the temple. He was what would now be called "a theistic humanist." Since his contact with God was very theoretical, he felt that he had done well by himself, well by others, and well by God. The modern humanist is just as likely to be found outside the temple as in the temple, but he too, if he is a theist, has only a theoretical contact with God, and he feels that he has done well by others, well by himself, and well by God.

The negativism of Christ's day was made articulate by the theocratic and political leadership of the community. The negativism of a modern democracy is expressed through the indifference of the great middle class. The hypocrisy of Christ's day expressed itself through ecclesiastical legalism. The hypocrisy of our own day expresses itself through a shallow sentimentalism. But it's all the same hypocrisy, and all the same humanism, and all the same negativism.

3   MATERIALISM

Materialism is like negativism in that it is a trait of human behavior which does not start as a rounded philosophy, but which, given time, congeals into one until it threatens to engulf the outlook of a whole society. Theoretical materialism is avowed in the Soviet Union as a working system under the control of the state. We reject all such materialistic theory, but, like most nations in the day of their prosperity, we live under the sway of a materialism which is practical and unseen.

Americans have a great capacity for divorcing theory from practice, and possess only a slight taste for the intellectual and philosophical approaches. Materialism in this country is an unthinking practice, all the more subtle because it is unthinking, and having no less a profound effect upon people's thought because it has no thoughtful basis of its own.

Let us be sure that we know what we mean by the word. Materialism is not just a love of money, or of business success, although it may be related to those things. Materialism is any habit, either of thought or of conduct, which reduces life to a material basis, minimizing the spiritual part of man's nature. When a man is a materialist, he starts out by possessing things, and ends by having things possess him.

Materialism differs from humanism, in that the intellectuals and the *literati,* as a rule, have no more part in it than does the common man. In spite of the common belief that the theories of the left-wing intellectuals have a corrosive effect upon any spiritual view of life, the non-intellectual promotes materialism just as readily as does the intellectual.

In the home where materialism reigns, one is typically confronted with a father and mother who would be shocked at the thoughts expressed in left-wing literature, but who, for their own part, seem incapable of even elementary ambitions toward the knowledge of God. Church members, doubtless; but take away the overstuffed furniture, the television, the splendid car, and there wouldn't be much left.

Of course, not everyone who owns overstuffed furniture, television, and a car is a materialist. What minister cannot recall a family who once had all these things, and more besides, who lost nearly everything they owned, but who showed they were not materialists by going right on in prayer, with honor and an increased depth of character? "Man shall not live by bread alone." [7] But such are not in the majority.

The spiritual disease created by widespread materialism plagues our churches. People for whom the things of the spirit are a foreign language take their spiritual poverty to church with them. Just as they cannot live at home without certain possessions, so they cannot stand church without forensic sermons and elaborate choirs. When simple, honest, straightforward religion is presented to them with love, as it is found in the New Testament, they are either amazed or bored. Open antagonism would not be as harmful as these people's inability to set their hearts toward God and Jesus Christ.

Open antagonism is at least the breaking up of the hard crusts which stifle the soul. It is at least a response, even if not the desired one. The antagonism sometimes is permanent and mortal, but sometimes also it is a modern instance of the son who at first said, "I will not," and who afterward changed his mind and did his father's will. [8]

Unhappily the Church, humanly considered, has viewed antagonism with a magnifying glass and patted boredom on the back. This has sometimes been accomplished by abandoning the direct teaching of religious truths. In doing this the Church has avoided conflict with the people of only shallow religious interests, but she has failed to meet the needs of those who come with spiritual hunger. Out of this trend came the disparagement of doctrine as something "un-Christian," the uncritical statement that "Christianity and Democracy are one and the same thing," and the substitution of "personality" for faith.

When it comes to taking the Gospel to the poor and the

[7] Matthew 4:4.   [8] Matthew 21:29.

bruised, our souls are emptied, our minds are fogged, and our hands are palsied by the emptiness of what we are doing with those who are not materially poor.

The poor are not all saints in the making by any means. Even when they are not, they are bringing children into the world terribly handicapped in many ways, needing, therefore, the healing touch, the loving guidance of Christ the Good Shepherd. We cannot be the agents in this work and at the same time operate the rest of our ministry in the materialist manner. The conflicts there are too great.

Materialism has fastened itself upon our national society to a far greater extent than have humanism and negativism. We, therefore, are confronted with larger quantities of it in the Church itself. If we are to be watchmen against materialism it is all the more important to begin at home: to be sure, doubly sure, that in the conduct of our own churches, we are pleasing God, in prayer, to the best of our ability. If we are praying first and acting in obedience afterward, we need not worry whether there is the right content in our worship and in our relations to our people; but there will be conflicts to face between what God wants of us and what seems to be expected of us from other quarters.

In the task of being watchmen against materialism in society at large, let us remember a few simple certainties. First, and most obvious, it is bad theology to teach that matter is evil. The trouble is not with matter, but with man's putting matter in a place of priority which does not belong to it. It is the human will that is wrong. What man does with matter is the thing which does the damage. "Do not lay up for yourselves treasures on earth, where moth and rust consume and where thieves break in and steal, but lay up for yourselves treasures in heaven, where neither moth nor rust consumes and where thieves do not break in and steal. For where your treasure is, there will your heart be also." [9]

Second, and less obviously, some of the preaching against materialism has made the mistake of blaming the factory system and the extensive use of machinery, as though the necessity of working with machines somehow infects a man with the sin of materialism. This is a little naïve. It involves the implication that agricultural workers can be much more spiritual than factory workers. Where is there evidence to support such a theory?

It also misses the real locus of the temptation, which is at the consumer end of the line, rather than at the manufacturing end. The only sense in which the factory system increases materialism is the sense in which it makes available to people such a high standard of material living that they are more strongly tempted to put their hearts and souls into material possessions. In so far as a man is both a factory worker and a consumer, it is as a consumer that he is tempted, not as a factory worker.

From this standpoint, the depression and the second world war were not an unmixed evil for this country. They did not make people as a whole more spiritual, but they introduced a healthy wedge of skepticism into the American faith in possessions. At least in a worldly way, we now know that possessions can destroy the civilization which produced them, unless they are intelligently managed for the good of society as a whole. In other words, things must always be truly possessed by the total nature of man, including his spiritual and intellectual insight. The moment goods become the possessor of man, instead of the things possessed by man, they are a destroying force.

[9] Matthew 6:19–21.

Sometime in 1929, an officer of a large business house engaged some friends in a conversation about his philosophy of business. The burden of his message was that American business had found the formula whereby money makes money. With this formula properly applied, prosperity, once started, generates and perpetuates itself, so that wealth can be made to increase in arithmetical, sometimes in geometrical progression. His thesis was not wholly selfish, because he went on to add that it was the mission of this country to pass on that formula to other countries, so that the whole world might be set on the path of permanent and increasing prosperity.

His friends, not being economists, listened and were impressed, but within a few months the depression came as though overnight. The business house of which this man was an officer was obliged to discharge most of its office force, and just managed to hang onto its own existence.

Through experiences like this, and through the growing understanding of such terms as "depression," "inflation," "price control," and "stabilization of wages," the public became aware of the fact that the economy needs to be controlled by just as complicated a system of checks and balances as does the government, if it is not to plunge the country into ruin.

Such a worldly consideration is the beginning of a dialectic of experience which can lead to a more spiritual view of life on the part of some, if we make the right use of it.

The New Testament is full of teachings of Christ designed to help people keep possessions in their place. There is the parable of the man whose ground brought forth plentifully, and who said to his soul: "Soul, you have ample goods laid up for many years; take your ease, eat, drink, be merry." There is the answer to the young man who desired spiritual perfection, and who was told to sell all that he had and give to the poor. Again, there is the teaching in the Sermon on the Mount. "Give to him who begs from you, and do not refuse him who would borrow from you." [10]

Since the coming of the depression of the thirties and the increasing social application of the science of psychology, a demand for security has been voiced all over the land. When we examine into it we discover that the kind of security meant is economic and psychological security—things not to be despised, even from the spiritual point of view. But the theory that the feeling of insecurity is bad is a mistaken theory. Insecurity is uncomfortable, yes; but so is a toothache. The discomfort of a toothache has the function of sending us to the dentist. The discomfort of insecurity should have the function of sending us to God.

We can turn this outcry for security to good account, in connection with the Sermon on the Mount. It so happens that the Sermon on the Mount contains its own purpose clearly stated within it. When we pick up a modern book we are accustomed to looking for the purpose of the book in a preface, printed somewhere before page one. The Sermon on the Mount has what corresponds to a preface, but through the intervals and logic of presentation, as well as through the accidents of transmission, the preface is at the end, instead of at the beginning. Nevertheless we find there a clear statement of purpose, and that purpose turns out to be none other than that of showing us the way to security. "Every one then who hears these words of mine and does them will be like a wise man who built his house upon the rock; and the rain fell, and the floods came, and the winds blew and beat upon that house, but it did not fall,

[10] Luke 12:19; Matthew 19:21; 5:42.

because it had been founded on the rock. And every one who hears these words of mine and does not do them will be like a foolish man who built his house upon the sand; and the rain fell, and the floods came, and the winds blew and beat against that house, and it fell; and great was the fall of it." [11]

So when we feel insecure, we must realize that genuine security is purchased at a price and that its source and foundation are God. There is no ground for optimism, but there is firm ground for faith and hope.

4 COLLEGE AND UNBELIEF

Literary and academic ideologies, when they seem destructive, had best not be met directly. They are too prolific. Only some will take lasting root, and we are seldom in a position to judge the lasting ones ahead of time. After the example of Christ, we should not try to anticipate future ideologies, but should bend our energies against those which are presently active, thereby building up in the body spiritual an immunity toward future evils.

College students are engrossed in a struggling unbelief, due partly to their emergence into an unfamiliar religious and secular environment, and partly to their normal stage of physical and emotional development, never easy, and often entered into without sufficient or true preparation.

Let us set down a few of the rudiments of an apologetic. Since students, for the most part, are learning the scientific method, they expect all truth to be capable of absolute demonstration, by one person to another. They fail to realize that, even in

[11] Matthew 7:24–27.

scientific truth, this demonstrability is present only when the materials, as well as the sense perceptions, are available to both parties. For example, it is possible for a physicist to demonstrate to a student that water is composed of hydrogen and oxygen, because the materials for the demonstration, and the sense perceptions, are common to the teacher and the student. An explorer of ocean depths, on the other hand, could not demonstrate the habits of deep-sea fish to a man from Missouri, unless the man from Missouri were willing to go down in the bathysphere with him. Students hearing him lecture would have to take his word for it and be content with his descriptions.

Now spiritual truth, and the materials and perceptions for demonstrating it, are only available to those who have taken a certain journey, starting with a quantum of belief, and continuing in prayer based upon that belief. For those people the demonstration comes. For others it does not.

Why belief? Why cannot the journey be started on the basis of assured knowledge? Well, Saint Thomas Aquinas and modern psychology are both agreed that the intellect can know only through the senses, and "no man hath seen God at any time." Let us be agnostic, for the moment, in order not to beg the question. The concept of God is a comprehensive one. If this total reality were available to the senses, or to philosophy, the great philosophical endeavors of the past and the great scientific endeavors of the present would have discovered it by now. According to anthropologists, the size and physiological potential of the human brain has not increased in the past twenty thousand years.

Nor can logic give an absolute proof of God. Logic can afford absolute proof about things which are definable in terms of something else. This is especially true of mathematics, which is the language of definition of numbers, which, in turn, can be applied to the description of shapes, quantities, dimensions, weights, etc. Because it is a language of definition, mathematics is full of logical proofs. But the comprehensive concept cannot be defined in other terms. There are no other terms. Logic is stumped.

Therefore, when a college student asks a believer to prove the existence of God, the proof by demonstration is impossible because the spiritual "material" which is available to the believer is not available to the student. One can only say, "Take the journey and you will see." The proof by logic is out of the question because the concept of God is comprehensive.

This is all such a matter of common sense that the real deterrent is usually of another kind. A person struggling with unbelief is not tempted to take the step of initial belief because most of the believers he sees are believers only because they are too thoughtless to be anything else, in a society in which belief is traditional. They are not believers because they are trying to live a good life under difficulties. Therefore, in any effort to help people in their thoughts about the reality of God, we must be very sure that they know we are talking about a good God, who is the origin and the fulfillment of every high conviction.

Also, without knowing it, college students are Cathari, purists, looking for the perfect Church, holding to the childish principle that there is no such thing as a bad Christian. Finding the Church disappointing from this standpoint, they decide that they can be religious without the Church, sampling the nectar of various religious bodies as a bee samples flowers, though far more critically, and with far less industry.

Of course, a college student has not yet faced up to the whole truth about himself, or herself. Only when we realize how patient and merciful God must be with us, only then do we have the basis for being patient and merciful with others.

On the intellectual side, the clergy must cling to the principle employed by the high scholastics against the Cathari, namely, that there are good and there are bad Christians. This has always been so and it will always be so. The solution is found in the parable of the wheat and the tares.

5   THE HABIT OF DISSENT

Like academic unbelief, the habit of dissent is intimately related to our institutional life. Instead of the college, however, the Church is the institution in the background of the problem. Yet, as we shall see, the Church is also the institution most capable of offering a solution.

Out of the very nature of religious conviction springs the ability to say "No." Protestants have made decisions against, as well as for, statements of religious belief; and have made them with such firmness as to have separated into many denominations. Catholics also have the ability to say "No." Controls exercised over the reading and other activities of members are Catholic "Nos." It has been said that the ability to say "No" is one of the ingredients of maturity.

However, when "No" is said from force of habit, it ceases to serve life. Unlike the negativist, the dissenter loves life with great intensity in his chosen portion of it. The merely habitual "No" is usually an excuse to avoid encountering someone else's truth. One of the benefits of human society is that the individual encounters other areas of truth in addition to his own, and is given an opportunity to grow in these areas. That, though, requires humility, perhaps also some self-effacement and pain. It is so costly that dissent looks attractive as a means of escape. This dissent by habit is intertwined with the dissent of honest conviction, so that it is difficult to talk about one without talking about the other.

In the field of religion, Protestantism has given full respect to the principle of honest dissent, yet even apart from the ecumenical movement Protestants have known that their negatives of dissent have as their only legitimate end the preaching of the positive Gospel of Christ. The ecumenical movement may be looked upon as an exploration of regions of dissent to see whether some that seemed to be necessary ought not to be treated as habitual. Haste and short cuts can do great damage here, because the One Church can never be the product of abandoned convictions.

As long, however, as Christ is being preached each Christian is challenged to advance, by grace, into the whole of life as God has made it. He must not use the habit of dissent as an excuse to keep his encounter with life within the narrow limits of his own vision and comfort. This affects the Christian as a person and as a contributor to society. Even though Christianity has not succeeded in keeping the actuality of the one, visible Church, it is still a religion according to the whole man; that is, according to total human personality.

When we turn our gaze from the religious world to the secular world, we find the same dissidence at work. People are not content to be specialists in the co-operative sense in which St. Paul expressed that principle for the Church. "For as in one body we have many members, and all the members do not have the same function, so we, though many, are one body in Christ, and individually members one of another." [12]

[12] Romans 12:4, 5.

Instead of being co-operative specialists people have slipped into an *ex parte* view of life, in which there is a wall of distrust between types of personality and between different professions in life. The scientist puts forth theories resulting from his work as though they represented a total view of life. The public relations man becomes an anti-intellectual. The business executive gives his attention to nothing serious outside of his own sphere. The artist depicts abstruse moods, proud of the fact that nobody but himself knows what they mean. The intellectual diagrams life safely removed from its flow.

This tendency to segregate ourselves by temperaments and professions grows worse as the community grows larger. In a small town the mutual contact among people of different types has not broken down as much as in the larger cities. It is a tenable speculation that our best fiction draws its material from small town life more easily and effectively because there a more nearly complete cross section of the human scene is available.

However, our world is now predominantly a world of big cities, where specialized organization creates artificial communities for each type and profession. If specialized organization is not present, mere numbers facilitate a natural segmentation. Of itself this typed community has its advantages. Doctors can share their common interests, as can the lawyers theirs and the businessmen theirs and the clergy theirs. Rather than criticize it we need only to give warning that one of its undesirable byproducts is a partly distintegrated community which no longer offers its daily challenge to the whole personality of the man and of the woman.

Christianity is a powerful antidote for this tendency when taken in its integrity. There is something down-to-earth and whole about Peter, the commercial fisherman, becoming a missionary, or the author of the fourth Gospel telling his religious story in philosophical terms, or Luke, the physician, becoming a religious historian. This life-according-to-the-whole is rightly called "catholic," because "catholic" means according to the whole. The word "wholesome" is another derivative of the same idea.

Yet, here again, religion is handicapped in this work of making life whole by the plague of sentimentality. We discussed sentimentality as a cloak for materialism. It needs also to be laid bare as the enemy of whole living, because it is based upon a schism between the emotions and the intellect.

Where sentimentality holds sway, religion is treated as something which happens entirely in the realm of the emotions. It has an intellectual dressing, to be sure, just as a window display, but really now it's a matter exclusively of the emotions.

Look, in your leisure moments, at representative teachings of Christ in the New Testament. They are, it is true, free from the academic approach. Everything is expressed in terms of the common life of all people, educated and uneducated. But they are packed with solid intellectual content. There is a firm logic, an appeal to common sense. There is even, especially in the parables, an application of the business principles of this world to the spiritual principles of the Kingdom of God.

There is sentiment there too, but sentiment which is deep and true, related always to appropriate action and sacrifice. "Greater love has no man than this, that a man lay down his life for his friends." [13]

So, in Christ, sentiment and intellect are integrated into a perfect whole; and we can truly say that Christianity, rightly understood, is religion according to the whole personality: i.e.,

[13] John 15:13.

it is catholic with respect to the total life of a man, as well as with respect to the whole faith.

Because the Church, on her human side (and this goes for some bearing the name "Catholic," as well as for Protestants), has acceded to the segmentation of life and of human personality which we find in modern society, she has necessarily fallen into the trap of alienating one group while catering to the other.

The excellence of the ancient hymns of the church is due to the fact that in them there is a beautiful blending and integrating of the intellect with the emotions.

So modern society, beginning with an easy dissent, and continuing to generate schismatic groups in secular as well as in religious life, has produced a conflict within the human personality, so that a man is no longer a whole man, and the design of life is broken up artificially into a strange sort of puzzle, without any total meaning.

6   THE LOST SENSE OF HOLINESS

One ideological tendency current today has long been with us in disguise, and we are especially aware of it now only because it has at last dropped its disguise. That is the loss of a sense of holiness.

The sense of holiness is not the same thing, quite, as the sense of awe. The sense of awe can be aroused by many stimuli, a hurricane, a volcanic eruption, or a snow-capped mountain. But the sense of awe in connection with the sense of holiness is only a derivative. The sense of holiness itself is a recognition of value in an object, in particular the value of perfection, seen from the point of view of one's own imperfection. The only proper object for such a sense is God, who, alone, is free from imperfection; who, alone, is good.

Now Christianity teaches man a twofold doctrine about his own relation to perfection, from the standpoint of practical conduct. First of all, it teaches him that, just as God is not far off, but is immanent in man's being, so God's perfection is not far off, but is immanent as a potentiality in man's nature. "You, therefore, must be perfect, as your heavenly Father is perfect." [14]

On the other hand, Christianity teaches that a *sine qua non* of man's making good this potentiality is a recognition of his actual imperfection. The way to go down to your house justified is to learn to say, "God, be merciful to me a sinner!" [15]

And there is more to this second principle than meets the eye. It is not only that man is in danger of becoming blind to his own sin. It is also that, in so far as a man is good, he has that goodness only by sharing in the goodness of God. It is spiritually fatal to balance our sins against our virtues, because our virtues, in so far as they do exist, are of God and not of ourselves.

So God, who is absolute perfection and original goodness, is not only transcendent, He is also immanent in us, and his perfection exists in us as a potentiality for complete goodness which is hindered from realization only by our sin.

It is the immediate, spontaneous perception of this double truth which is involved in the sense of holiness. It is awareness, on the one hand, of the disparity between God's perfection and our imperfection, and, on the other hand, of the compelling shame of that disparity, which can be healed only by God's help

[14] Matthew 5:48.   [15] Luke 18:13.

and mercy. "Woe is me! for I am undone; because I am a man of unclean lips, and I dwell in the midst of a people of unclean lips: for mine eyes have seen the King, Jehovah of hosts." [16]

A very important clause in this passage is the last clause, "for mine eyes have seen the King." In other words, the sense of the holy is not an examination of conscience without any objective basis for that examination. It is not the result of a person's turning in on himself. It is the result of an objective perception, an objective vision. "For mine eyes have seen the King, Jehovah of Hosts."

Now it is true that we are not all given special visions, but the perception on which the sense of the holy is based is a perception which is a normal endowment of human nature. It lay behind both the attraction and the repulsion which Christ caused in people. They perceived his holiness; and those of good will, who wanted a still better will, were attracted to it. Those of evil will were repelled by it, but all recognized it.

When we cease to exercise this natural endowment we are truncating human nature just as surely as when we cease to exercise the intellect or the emotions in any other field, and we are slamming the door on one of the God-given avenues of spiritual living.

What has happened to the sense of the holy in our own day? The usual theory is that the acids of intellectual criticism have destroyed so many objects of reverence that man has ceased to be able to revere any object, including God.

It seems to me that this theory has a fatal weakness, in that it confesses that there are some objects of reverence which cannot stand against acid truth. By the very way in which it is stated, the theory reveals its false premise, because any object

[16] Isaiah 6:5.

worthy of man's reverence is one which can stand the acid test. Is not this theory, therefore, a product of the false sentimentality which we have been thinking about?

Therefore, it is better to say that in the past man's sense of the holy has been directed to merely human objects, and that these objects have, one by one, become the cause of disillusionment. Now we are in the sad state of thinking that disillusionment is a bad thing, not realizing that no sane person wants to put his faith in an illusion anyway. Religion, on the other hand, directs the sense of the holy to its only proper object, which is God; who stands up under the acid test, does not produce disillusionment, and who rewards the sense of the holy with a vision, a purpose in life, and a genuine basis for repentance and peace.

It will do no good to rail against the loss of respect, the loss of the sense of the holy toward what we once called "the established institutions," which have an authority and a good derived only from God. What will do good is to recover the vision of God and to redirect the sense of the holy to that only worthy vision.

The worship of the Church is the focal point at which the Christian community renews its grasp of this high purpose. Such, however, is the force of the ideological tides discussed in this chapter that worship tends to be a mere adjunct of the Church's program, instead of the source from which the program is derived.

The optimism whereby we put all disaster in the past, the humanism whereby we trust ourselves with our own salvation, these tides are expressed in the drive for numbers above all else and the measuring of success solely in terms of bustle and enthusiasm. Materialism asks for this dilution too, and for magnificent buildings and equipment without much thought about what the people are to be like, from God's point of view, who administer and use this equipment. These things constitute the watchman's task. He must give warning before it is too late for the Church to reverse the tide, and to begin reacting for good upon the world.

Chapter 7

TOWARD CYNICISM

The attitudes reviewed in the preceding chapter were the natural products of success. When we are successful and surrounded by prosperity we are more prone to be optimistic humanists, or lazy negativists, or seekers of material comforts, or disparaging of belief, or easy dissenters, and generally neglectful of God. However, when these attitudes are indulged beyond the point of success they produce reactions of an unpleasant kind. In this chapter we shall try to review the unpleasant reactions. That is the reason for the title "Toward Cynicism." The word "toward" stands for the fact that these reactions are directional rather than absolute. The word "cynicism" stands for the fact that they represent a rejection of the old idealism.

1 THE TWO LEVELS

This movement toward cynicism is taking place in two levels of our culture. In the uppermost cultural level all are aware of it in theology, in literature, in the arts, and in politics. The open and articulate character of the movement as expressed in these media allows us to review this evidence briefly, in order to devote more time to the subtler evidence from the other level, that of public opinion generally.

In theology the reaction against spiritual optimism has

found expression in several ways: the re-emphasis on the doctrine of original sin, the return to a sharpened view of revelation as against the older confidence in man's natural powers of religious search, and the pointing up of "encounter" and "decision," giving the religious life a quality of crisis in contrast to the older emphasis on natural growth.

These tendencies in theology cannot be called "cynicism," for —given belief in God—one can be disillusioned with the older faith in human ideals without becoming cynical. When the disillusionment occurs *without* religious belief then the results may roughly be summarized by the term "cynicism."

Thus, in literature, the great vogue enjoyed after the twenties by the essays of H. L. Mencken and the realistic novels of Theodore Dreiser and Sinclair Lewis was evidence of interest in what we might call the obverse of the coin, that harsh, factual and disconcerting side of life which idealism had sought unsuccessfully to conceal. This literary trend has continued in the meantime in such quantity as to constitute a tradition free to exploit the themes of disillusionment and meaninglessness.

Recently, also, the French novelist and essayist, Albert Camus, has extended his influence in America through translations of many of his works. Equipped with an artful and convincing style, Camus portrays the futility of life's drives, which aim at goals never to be reached. He sees shallow unreality in the traditional middle-class pieties, but neither does he have any faith in the dialectic of revolt, which ultimately destroys the freedoms it thought to create.

In the visual arts similar symptoms are evident, where painters and sculptors abandon the ideal form in favor of the disintegrated and the grotesque.

Finally, our political outlook has been chilled by the impact of the second world war and the development of atomic weapons. The challenge of our national strength by the Soviet Union but caps the climax of our growing fear. Because this political mood is publicized by the communicative arts it deserves to be treated with the other articulate evidences from literature and the visual arts.

All these "signs of the times" are easy to read because they are spelled out and displayed in public. They are taking place in what we referred to above as the uppermost level of our culture.

But we also said that the movement toward cynicism is taking place on another level, that of the less articulate but far more numerous populace at large. That is the mass of the people among whom all are numbered who are not renowned theologians nor famous novelists nor political leaders. They, too, have been carried, sometimes unknowingly, away from the older faith in ideals.

The task of reviewing such a change in the popular mood is a difficult one. The evidences for it must be gleaned from public events, which are subject to various interpretations, or from the personal experience of the observer, which is evidentially valid only in so far as it is common to most other observers. Nevertheless the task must be attempted by the watchman: the people for whose sakes he gives his warnings are caught up in this change of mood the more powerfully because it is submerged and so difficult to identify.

2   THE SOLID CITIZEN

While we may differ in details about the evidences for the growth of popular cynicism, most would agree, in general, that "the great American middle class" has not been itself since the 1930s. For example, the "New Deal" could hardly have obtained such majority support at the polls without the backing of large segments of conservative opinion, in addition to liberal opinion. That is to say that some conservatives shared a view that would have been untenable for them a decade earlier.

Also, the attitude of the solid citizen toward his role as a voter is more down-to-earth, less idealized than formerly. He may think of his vote as a responsibility or a duty, but always with his attention upon certain critical opinions of his own. He can no longer be patronized into making a dramatic pageant out of election day while a certain trusted few shoulder the decisions. He is patriotic, but since the depression, and more especially since the second world war, his patriotism is of the hardpan variety.

3   SHOCK LANGUAGE, MORALS AND BELIEF

A hardening of mental attitudes is also reflected in the increasing prevalence of shock language. Not too long ago, the shocking word, the self-conscious use of coarse expressions in public speech, were confined to those who have always found profanity the most accepted idiom of communication in their group. The fact that the profane are not always the true does not alter the fact that a hunger for truth is often the motivation for the use of profanity as well as the mere need to conform. This group is hardly productive of a change of public attitude because this group is always with us, even in times of idealism.

A second group is more symptomatic of change. These are the people of reasonably cultivated background who, on the surface, would have every reason to keep speech polite and smooth. When these cultivate the shock expression and manage to create movement in that direction, then the polite public itself has changed its mind. This symptom appeared first in the fringe few, those who might be expected to rebel as occasional "black sheep." The significant thing is that shock language is no longer a "black sheep" peculiarity. It has caught on. The language is increasingly enriched by it. It is seen by the general public to serve a purpose. It is no longer the special privilege of the profane. Obviously one of the pieties of the past has disappeared.

At first glance we are tempted to say that value is being destroyed and that the world is rapidly losing all its morals. However, historians of western culture are aware that polite language and morals bear little, if any, fixed relation to one another. Perhaps it is truer to say that historical examples show that public immorality can be at its worst when polite language is approaching its highest levels. One thinks of France at the time of Louis XIV. Conversely, impolite language can be at its lowest level when morals are at their highest. The Bible is the prime example of this. But for the fact that we have become immunized to its full meanings, the language of portions of the Bible would sometimes be unreadable in public. It is, linguistically, a shocking book. Saint Jerome and Martin Luther are handy examples of Christians of high moral principles who found coarse and shocking language useful.

The long view reveals to us that the strict canons which limit all social expression to polite and delicate language are extremely recent in our culture. Therefore, when these canons of delicacy are flouted, we should understand this as a return to the historically usual, rather than as the introduction of something unusual. Furthermore the moral implications of the change are too complex to be judged, out of hand, as a movement away from morality. We can only take it on the surface as a symptom of public cynicism, in the sense of a disillusionment with older social ideals, a collapse of confidence in the pious.

Connected with this change in the proprieties of language is a change in attitude toward religious belief. We are not here thinking of the problem of unbelief as such, but of the public acknowledgment of this problem. Throughout the first three decades of the century the problem was aired quite freely in academic and theological circles, but in so far as church congregations were concerned, the laity were largely passive. The non-churchman politely kept his thoughts to himself, except for the occasional "radical." Now, this too is changing. Laymen feel less passive in matters of belief. No longer need one fear to express unbelief to a clergyman. No longer are believers obliged to leave the active defense of belief to their clergy. It is rarely true today that a person's job is jeopardized by deviation from the religious norm. The clergy are less and less immune to challenge in public. The Church's apologetics must now compete in an open market. Too much has happened to destroy the former confidence in the institution and in the tradition as a source of security. "Change and decay" is too visible. He who changes not is, therefore, more actively believed in or disbelieved in, and more openly debated.

An attempt to soften the edges of this emerging problem was for a time seen in certain literary devices. It is easy in the sermon or in religious literature to concentrate on spiritual ideals so as to divert attention from the question whether these ideals can survive in nature or whether there is a God who will sustain them. Such "illusions of immortality" are to be understood as a rear-guard action. They cannot represent any more than a backward look. At their worst they exploit a wistful populace.

The development of the language of shock and the emergence into the open of the problem of unbelief have afforded us evidence of a quiet but powerful undertow in the ocean of public opinion. Now people as a whole are involved, not just the articulate few. No longer can we isolate or ignore the occasional cases within our congregation or community.

First let us examine the more tangible movements on the surface of our society. Whether they be symptom or disease, cause or effect, we cannot always tell. The fact that they are happening is what interests us. They show direction.

4 MIGHT MAKES RIGHT

"Might makes right" is a principle we all are happy with when we have the might. The wonderful thing about these three words is that, without any risk, we can reverse the statement into "right makes might." This reversible statement satisfies both poles of our psychological need. We need power, but we also need justification. "Might makes right; right makes might" suited Americans perfectly a generation ago. We were powerful, but we were also good. It was more pleasant to think that we were powerful because we were good, but in the presence of any threat we could also say that we were good because we were powerful.

This comfortable position we no longer enjoy. We can no longer equate "might" with "right" without making responsible and painful choices. We are discovering that they cannot be combined in a statement reversible at will. In our life within the nation two struggles illustrate this: the struggle between unions and management and the struggle for law enforcement.

In thinking about the struggle between unions and management, we should be sure to distinguish the lawful from the unlawful elements in the situation, even when they appear to illustrate the same trend. As a lawful movement, the establishment of the principle of collective bargaining has forced us to take a truer view of the might-right relationship. It is obvious that the word "collective" in the phrase "collective bargaining" is equivalent to the word "power." Collective bargaining is power bargaining in the sense that the worker has found a device which prevents him from being hopelessly outpowered in his relations with his employer. Otherwise it was inevitable that the employer, in our large-company system, should become the worker's overlord. He might be a beneficent overlord, but still an overlord.

However, American idealism did not use as its historic model the revolts of the peasants in the fourteenth century, but that earlier revolt of the barons against the king which produced *Magna Carta*. It was easy to de-emphasize the barons' use of force, and the fact that they were powerful individuals, in order to idealize the rights confirmed by *Magna Carta,* and to imag-

ine that these rights were established in the interests of all the
people.

Without seeming to realize the partial parallel, we have par-
ticipated in our own day and in our own country in a revolt of
workers against employers. Certain rights have been established, not by an appeal to some abstract moral law, but by
application of power on behalf of assumed rights, after the
workers had found a way, through organization, of matching
the power of the employers.

Here is a winning of rights too close in time and place to be
idealized. Obviously might confirmed right. Clearly, we can no
longer refer all struggles for rights to past history where they do
not embarrass us. We are forced to watch the process repeated
in our midst, where we cannot view it romantically. Might and
right are seen not to be reversible. We are forced to accept the
fact that might confirms right.

As is to be expected, the momentum of the application of
might carries it beyond the acceptance point of society's laws.
Consequent upon the achievement of the practice of lawful collective bargaining has come the experience with power in the
hands of law-defying individuals. It does no good to call them
names. They have no scruple with respect to the total community. Their use of power in certain areas of the labor movement
has revealed them as destroyers of the whole. They use the
needs and money of the workers, not to humanize life for others
but to aggrandize themselves. Society is obliged to react against
them as a menace. It summons its own force in defense of its
own lawful procedures. Again the old idealism has been dealt a
blow. Repressive power is seen as the only defense against law-
less leadership.

Quite apart from the labor movement is the struggle with the increase in local crime. We like to call this "juvenile delinquency." Presumably it is "juvenile" because its perpetrators are young and seem to be getting younger. It is "delinquency" because we feel obliged, in this scientific age, to psychologize crime.

As a destruction of the old ideals, this community experience with juvenile delinquency attacks us on many fronts. It shows that we are not the classless society we thought we were. It shows that, left to his own devices, the citizen is not automatically benefited by this beneficent society. It shows that fear has its constructive uses. These three discoveries, resulting from the experience with crime, are all reversals of the idealistic tradition.

Surely American orthodoxy has been teaching us that, while our society may be specialized, its only class stratification is a voluntary one. It has supposed that given a beneficent community and humanitarian government the beneficial response of the citizenry would be broken only by the occasional nonconformist, not by significant groups. Finally, sweet reasonableness, it has been argued, is the only valid approach.

In the last two of these principles, American orthodoxy has felt itself superior to religious orthodoxy, which lays as great a weight upon response to a gift as it does upon the gift; and which never omits the principle of the fear of God.

Who would hold today that the only class stratification within our society is voluntary? It seems perfectly clear that crime is at least partly due to dissatisfaction with an underling status. It is true that the wrong choices and bad or no training must be added to the basic dissatisfaction in order to produce crime. However, it is demonstrably not true that opportunities are equal, in the United States or anywhere else. Nor does nature cause all the gifted children to be born into situations favoring the development of their gifts.

The prison chaplain, the policeman, and the social worker in a depressed neighborhood can quickly strip us of any illusions on this point. It is indeed a miracle when children born into the bottom class ever achieve a stable relationship to the world around them, or to themselves. Any youngster with ability or gumption finds himself in a world of closed doors; closed doors which spell insanity or revolt. The observer from the more privileged sections may well despairingly conclude that a return to the ancient system of bondage, which we sneeringly call "slavery," might not be so bad after all. Was it worse to be bought and sold than to be psychologically destroyed? At least a gifted bond servant might be schooled at the master's expense and might tutor the master's child.

The second of the shattered illusions is that a beneficent society will draw grateful response from all but a tiny few of the benefited citizens. Were the grateful response of the citizenry to shrink too radically, democracy as a working system would come to an end. The fact that democracy is still a working philosophy in this country proves that the idea of co-operative interaction is still reasonably strong. We rightly cling to it as essential to our way of life.

However, the deterioration has begun. When crime ceases to be the aberration of an individual and begins to be the common recourse of large numbers of underprivileged youngsters with minimal expectations from life, an obvious community sickness confronts us. Crime waves, in contrast to individual crime, are symptomatic of a corrosion of our way of life. The grateful response is missing from a significant segment of society. We must conclude that either the society has not been so beneficent as we thought, or the response is not so confidently to be expected.

Finally, the liberal-American conviction that sweet reasonableness is always the right approach to the lawbreaker is losing ground. Community experience with crime, both juvenile and adult, is slowly educating us to the realization that the appeal to truth by way of the friendly and the reasonable enjoys only an indifferent success at the very best. At the more usual worst, it walks into the trap of the skilled deceiver.

When we take this examination of American illusions a step further, we observe that two secondary ideals have turned out to be equally fallacious. The first of these is that the emotion of fear is always a destructive emotion, and the second is that sincerity prevents falsehood.

A generation ago there was widespread propaganda to the effect that fear is always bad. The late President Franklin D. Roosevelt made a popular pronouncement when he declared that the only thing we need to fear is fear itself. *The Book of Common Prayer* is less popular but more profound when it lists "the spirit of holy fear" among the gifts prayed for at Confirmation. The popular mood had a half-truth on its side in its sweeping rejection of fear. The half-truth is that human personality develops better with the co-operative and forward-looking moods of Saint Paul's trilogy, "faith, hope and love." It made the mistake, however, of supposing that these constructive moods were self-validating. That is, that if only we learn to generate these moods from within, we have thereby the power to convert bad situations into good situations, bad decisions into good decisions, ignorance into knowledge, and so on. Fear, as the opposite mood, was considered to be inevitably deadly and wrong.

One inkling that we had made a mistake about this came from the professional psychiatrists. They have been telling us, on the authority of extensive observation, that an inevitable ingredient in the character of mature people is precisely a certain fear. The person who is "mature," in the sense that he has entered into a beneficial and stable give-and-take with his fellows, is quite capable of fear. He respects the right and wrong qualities of situations. He is not indifferent about decisions. He knows that such securities as he may enjoy are relative, and may come to an end at any time. In other words, fear itself is not the only thing we need to fear. The absence of fear may be much more ominous. There is such a thing as "holy" fear.

When a proper understanding of fear is applied to the problem of massive crime, a first step has been taken toward a solution. A fearful community will discipline itself into action to correct degrading living conditions, and will in turn teach discipline to its citizens. When we see the problems of crime in this light, it is clear that true reason is fearful, as well as sweet.

As for sincerity, who would have thought, even a decade ago, that it would soon cease to be valuable as a criterion of useful relationships? We had supposed that, given sincerity in both parties, a constructive relationship would generally ensue. We knew, of course, that insanity was full of useless sincerity, but it did not occur to us that sane, active, and successful participants in society can likewise be sincere and untruthful at the same time. The nearest we came to drawing this conclusion was but a vague disquietude acquired from our lay contacts with professional psychiatry. We gathered only dimly from popular presentations of psychiatry that the sincere and the untrue often go together. To be sure, an occasional skeptic would impugn the validity of the common attitudes about ourselves and would extend his skepticism into moral indifferentism, but we disposed of him by calling him a "radical."

When we moved beyond such special situations, however, we were quite sure that sincerity and truth were, for all practical purposes of normal living, sufficiently close together. We were in need of the concept of sincerity as an antidote to the sin of hypocrisy and, since hypocrisy is the religious and political disease *par excellence*, we built up large reserves of sincerity in the interests of a trustworthy church and a trustworthy society. Afterward, this same criterion of sincerity was thought universally applicable to individual relationships as well.

What we failed to realize was that a man can be a sincere fool, a sincere schemer, and even a sincere liar. Sincerity only tells us about a person that he has convinced himself. It does not tell us whether the conviction in question meets any of the other criteria of truth.

Furthermore, when we ask what other criteria of truth there are, we either get into the world of fundamental skepticism where only the professional philosopher is at home, or we retreat into our own complacent sincerities, or we accept a state of real confusion. Since the courts of law are obliged to function without waiting for the community to develop a perfect philosophy of human nature, it is in the operations of the courts that the findings of psychiatry have entered our common thinking and have ceased to be a fringe concern, or the speculations only of an occasional "radical."

5 EDUCATION AND THE COMMUNITY

Not only in the experiences of our courts have the former ideals been modified, but in the area of public education. Our lofty ambition of making America "a land of equal opportunity for all" has necessarily committed us to a system of universal education. That this system has been a boon to human values and to the survival fitness of our democratic system cannot be denied. The fact that we are at odds with one another over theories of pedagogy is rather a good sign than a bad. The great corrective for all pedagogical sins is the confrontation with actual fact. Whether a school be adjudged "too old-fashioned" or "too advanced" is less important than the experience which the system has with actual children, meeting a growing situation in a competitive society. Were our theoretical mistakes the only problem, the public school system might be one social function in which the old ideals could be maintained against creeping cynicism.

However, we are not so fortunate. Schools, especially in the large cities, are overcrowded and underdisciplined. Our troubles stem in large part from the size of the task. School boards are obliged to compromise with the political community on the one hand and with the pupil community on the other, almost to the point of the breakdown of the system. New buildings and rising teachers' salaries require more money than the political community is willing to pay. The compromise with the pupils is of another kind. When children come together from radically different neighborhoods and home attitudes, the task of co-ordinating them into a working group demands more leadership than is often available. Only the rarely gifted principal, helped by a better-than-average staff, and backed by a determined community, can hope to produce an effective school under such circumstances. Of these three ingredients, the third is most frequently absent. If the determined community were not absent, the problem would not exist; no integrated community would ask its school administrators to attempt such a miracle as most of our schools must attempt in the absence of public support.

Out of this experience with universal education, therefore, comes another shock to the old ideals. How noble was the thought that our country was to be a land of equal opportunity for all, the melting pot for the distressed of many nations, a classless society devoted to freedom, hence the experimental station where all that is precious and of human value was to be developed. Presumably then, the rest of the world was to learn these methods and values from us. This would make us the new nation under God, chosen to lead the world out of its past mistakes. Now we are not so sure. In the public schools, where the ideal is faced in its most fleshly form, the task is proving too big, too complicated. Not only is the task too big, but we also are proved unready.

Linked with our public education problems is the struggle over racial integration. Because the problem is so obtrusive the struggle needs to be reduced to size if we are to give it its proper place as a symptom. It is not a trend so much as a painful awareness of an unspanned breach in our society which has always been there, but which we had managed to ignore. Now that the Supreme Court decision has forced the issue in such an inescapable area as the public school system, we are merely getting down to business in a matter which we prefer not to think about.

Our reaction to the unhappy situation is too recent to be easily understood in its implications for the future. We are now looking eagerly for solutions and finding them hard to come by. We may suffer one more blow to our traditional confidence in the American way of life, or we may solve the problem and renew our hope.

From the standpoint of the old idealism, the old optimism, and the old humanism, the symptoms and experiences reviewed in this chapter represent a reversal of the public mood, at its worst destructive of the former attitudes. We have been careful to take our evidence from movements which involve the middle class as a whole. We have tried not to be distracted by the inflammatory extremes. Intentionally we have paid no attention to the volcanic excitement of and about the late Senator Joseph McCarthy, and have drawn only cautious and limited conclusions from the controversy over racial integration.

The deep direction of the tide itself is the watchman's real concern. He sees it running out. With appropriate cynicism, yet also with truth, we may describe our collective selves as a young, egotistical people making uncomfortable contact with the real world.

Chapter 8

<<<<<<<<<<<<<<<<<<<<<<<<<<<<<<<<<<<<<<<<<<<<<<

SOME POSITIVE TRENDS

Nature is kinder to our American society than we deserve. With all our drifting into disillusionment, which we examined in the preceding chapter, there are counter moods of a happier sort at work among us. The large-scale effort to make up the housing shortage which existed after the last war has changed the physical aspect of life for many, in such a way as to alter for the better their spiritual outlook. Cultural contacts with Europe and cultural interests at home have become the possession of many formerly excluded from those experiences, and several factors have combined to cause American families to cherish home life once again.

Then, too, there is the fact that those who have had reason to criticize the old faith in ideals now find themselves forced to adopt some kind of faith of their own, through the pressure of the necessities of life. Positives, therefore, are mixing with the negatives and to some extent are counteracting them.

1 NEW HOUSING

The spiritual impact of buying a new house is deceptively deep. The act of accepting responsibility for payments on a mortgage throughout a term of fifteen or twenty years is a sobering one. When the salaried member of the household signs away a significant portion of his earnings for a third of his adult life expectancy, he is under the necessity of taking positive attitudes toward life. He is forced to believe that more of his daily commitments—to his family, his work, and his friends—are worth the entering into and the struggle to maintain. He can no longer spend his time being bitter about the mistakes of the older generation. He must now run the risk of making his own mistakes. He can no longer discard all conservative habits. He has some values now of his own to conserve.

Under the housing lag produced by the second world war, an amazing number of Americans were living in old houses and old neighborhoods in which their own creative and responsible effort had little part. The spiritual trouble with the old house is not that it is old but that it is debt free. The spiritual trouble with the old neighborhood is not that it is old but that its values are defensive instead of dynamic.

When young married couples live in debt-free houses, even if they pay rent, they are renting shelter which was created and paid for by a past generation. A rented house is one which has no financial hold on the occupant from lease to lease, or even from month to month within a lease. The occupant can move at any time with no regret, as far as the shelter is concerned, but that of sentiment and convenience. His own planning, his own hard work, his long-term bookkeeping are in no way involved. The house was built before he was born. Its mortgage has long since been liquidated. Someone long ago planned it, worried over it, exulted over it, and finally, at long last paid for it. As an object of deep human concern the house is finished.

Therefore when the pressure of numbers and the desire for higher material standards drive us *en masse* to buy new houses in new developments we unwittingly send our roots deeper into the soil. The tremendous number of Americans who have assumed long-term debt in order to buy new homes represents a real reversal of the trend away from lasting values. Every couple which shares the struggle to create the physical ingredients of a home is bound to make more room for the spiritual ingredients as well. They are no longer using temporarily the leftover shelter created by someone else's toil, worry, and joy. They are doing their own planning, their own worrying, their own toiling, and looking for their own joy as an end-product.

The old neighborhood is the collective and spiritual counterpart of the old house. Again, the trouble with the old neighborhood is not that it is old, but that it is attempting to cling, defensively, to values established by someone else. Since those values are an end-product, they are not seen as compatible with the embarking of young families, but rather as endangered by them. The anxiety to defend the old against the new hinders the efforts of the new generation to create its own values. Younger people making fresh starts are not, thus, led to see the old neighborhood as a center of wisdom, but rather as the outworn remnant of a dying way of life.

Here, again, the older civilization of Europe seems able continually to vitalize its old neighborhoods with young life in a way which we Americans cannot. Necessity, rather than virtue, has again been the means. When there is no room for any other but the old neighborhood, age and youth have no choice but to continue to live together. It is now worth renewing the old house. It is now necessary to revitalize the old neighborhood. In these ways necessity has built a deeper civilization in Europe than expansive opportunity has built in the United States.

Until the same necessities are upon us, we must expect our old neighborhoods, like our old houses, to be bastions of the discarded rather than sources of wisdom. We must expect young life to go elsewhere and to learn its own wisdoms its own way. The fact that a mass movement into new housing developments has typified American family life over the past decade is, therefore, a spiritual as well as an economic and sociological fact. It is to be seen as nature's partial restoration of the balance between cynicism and the positive reaching out for life.

2 CULTURAL PENETRATIONS

New cultural interests have also begun to enter the American common life, the life of the predominant community. This spreading of an interest in things cultural through most of the levels of our population has been one product of our system of universal education, but it also has been greatly aided by the more even distribution of wealth. With increased physical well-being people have found ways to satisfy cultural needs which previously had been thought reserved for the favored few.

One can see the transformation taking place by watching the line of people waiting for admission to Carnegie Hall in New York City, or the Academy of Music in Philadelphia, or any musical auditorium anywhere in the country. A generation ago the best seats were bought up by patrons for "the season," while general admission lines were formed by worshipful followers of the prevailing musical cult. The "common people" did not belong either to the small group of patrons nor to a cult. Now see who goes to these affairs! It is harder and harder to find the patrons. It is harder and harder to draw the line between the members of a cult and the housewives, office workers, laborers, and other normal citizens. Citizens of the United States are at last taking their artistic enjoyments as a normal part of life.

This cultural penetration into the common life is taking place in the field of travel and international relations as well as in the fields of the better-known arts. Those who supply the food, clothing, shelter, and services are participating in the cultural life through their children, who, in increasing numbers, are studying French, German, Russian, Italian, or Spanish; who are beginning to travel abroad, and who are becoming the nation's schoolteachers and technicians.

This is a far cry from the former "melting pot" theory. By that theory we Americans were to absorb Europeans into our culture. Now the process is being reversed. Europeans are interesting us in their cultures. The significant factor in this change is its commonness, its penetrations of almost all the levels of our society. International exchange of interests is no longer a privilege reserved for an extremely selected elite.

This cross-fertilization provides an element of hope for the future of our democratic procedures because it means that the body of the people is acquiring a broader base of experience out of which to make political choices. The trend marks an important step away from the illusions of the ideal into the factual knowledge of the real for significant groups of voters. The old legends woven around the log-cabin-to-President and poor-boy-made-good themes served their day and in truth actually worked among an amazing number of people, thanks to the beneficent conditions provided by our wealthy democracy. However, in the process of our passing on from faith in legend to faith in the pragmatic fact our idealistic propaganda has undergone a healthy cynicism, a normal disillusionment, and a destruction of the cult out of which it sprang. We should be thankful for this change, in view of the hard road ahead for our country. Our thickening population, our loss of our once-precious isolation and of our material superiority, in short, our rapid plunge into the conditions which have affected the rest of the world, will not be manageable if our people continue to be blinded by the old illusions.

3 HOME AGAIN

Now that more Americans are escaping from the restrictions of the old cults, they are subtly taking more interest in their own homes. The recovery of home life in the United States is hard to believe in, because it flies in the face of what seems to be an overwhelming trend in the other direction. We are all so familiar with the complaint that the use of canned goods has destroyed the art of cooking and lowered the family significance, and that the movies have taken the place of entertainment within the home. And who has not felt that use of automobiles and the consequent freedom and rebelliousness of the younger generation has merely completed the destruction of home life? It is incredible but true that this situation is beginning to be reversed.

Television, new houses, and a changed psychology are three aids to this reversal which are obvious. The fact that moving-picture theaters have suffered a drop in business in spite of an increase in the population is a negative indication of the work of television in making entertainment available at home. The quality of motion pictures today is not radically worse nor better than in their day of prosperity, so that a measurable effect of television is the return of entertainment to the home.

We have already discussed the new house as a cause of deepened responsibility generally, but we can see it focused specifically as a return to home life. The physical labor and mental planning which go into changing the house and grounds as the builder left them into the house and grounds you really want constitute a very down-to-earth set of demands made upon you by your home. When you have put this much of yourself into it, you belong to it and it belongs to you. You have turned into a home-lover just when you thought you were emancipated from all such old-fashioned, frustrating ideas.

This takes us to the more vague, but equally real, psychological factor—the desire to be emancipated from old restrictions. This desire is never absent from human nature in any age, but it enjoyed special emphasis after the first world war. Even adult leaders in psychology and education supported the fight against artificial controls, and the struggle has continued into our mid-century decades. During this movement of emancipation, home ties were minimized. The time has come, however, for nature to assert itself. The illusion of salvation through controls had been counteracted by the illusion of boundless possibilities. When you fight one illusion with another illusion, both illusions die. More and more of the members of the emancipated generation are finding themselves face to face with the limits set by nature. They know now that they are in the same cycle of birth, home, insecurity, and death that their forebears experienced, and that they will never escape from the toils of this cycle. By the very nature of the case, freedom-seekers are accepting some facts, one of which is the home.

Chapter 9

PRESCRIPTIONS

If we really understood our Christian religion we would rejoice at the loss of faith in ideals, the exchange of sentiment for fact, and the discovery of the false in society. The Bible is not a book of ideals. It is a book about God. Nor is it a book for the parlor, where nothing unpleasant is said. Nor does it flatter society. It is precisely when we are forced, through inescapable fact, to face the horrid truths about life that this collection of sacred, though impious documents takes on a new vitality.

When we read the Bible with minds relaxed it turns out to be a heterogeneous series of writings containing cosmogony, religion, and politics in the large; in the small, all kinds of disaster, intrigue, crime, heroics, adventure, love, religious sacrifice, religious morals, miracles, rewards and punishments, divine intervention and prediction. The list could be extended much further and be better-arranged, but to extend it further and to arrange it better would not help describe the writings.

In order to describe the writings it would be necessary to note that this mixed collection of stories about human and divine activity is not like the *Arabian Nights,* nor *Alice in Wonderland,* though it has certain literary ingredients in common with these. It differs from them in that it takes itself seriously and, however clumsily, evolves certain themes about God and the world.

Let us set forth these themes. The Bible talks about a God who is. It is explicit that this God *is because he is,* not because some other being, through thinking or acting, made him be. It is rather that his thinking and his acting make other beings be. The world also is a consequence of his thoughts and actions, and as such is good. Yet, in varying degrees his creatures bear his image, and especially man. As made in God's image man can make real choices, not just staged choices, and the risk is run that the image will choose to substitute himself for the Person imaged. This is what has happened. The image is damaged because of his choosing to be a substitute god instead of a real image of the real God.

This is no mere theory but has had tangible consequences in the world. Nor is God indifferent about it. Through his special people, Israel, he has proclaimed himself, and has stated his requirements. Because he is not indifferent, his people know him to be holy. In fact this requiring side of God is what they understand by his holiness in addition to his awful majesty. He makes his prophets his spokesmen, sometimes against their will, and through them castigates his people, when they take advantage of the poor, are unkind to foreigners who visit them, disregard their obligations to one another, yet seek preferment from one another instead of from God, put on a religious act instead of being truly religious, or fail to set him above all else.

God also backs up his requirements by supporting action. He saves his people from tyranny in Egypt, gives them a guiding law and enters into a covenant with them. He also sustains them with the fruits of the earth and commands them to remember all that he has done for them—the escape from tyranny, and the enjoyment of the fruits of the earth—and to offer a sin offering, expecting even greater things in the future.

Greater things must be expected, because the law and the token offerings are temporary ends rather than cures for the sickness of man. Moreover Israel, after hundreds of years, enjoyed only a little glory as a kingdom before falling to a succession of more powerful nations and being dispersed through alien cultures.

In the Bible, as in all real life, the expected turns out to be the unexpected. A man of modest origin and a common name resumes God's self-proclamation, not only through his words but through his deeds, so much so that his followers come to know him as The Word, call him "Lord," and understand him and his prescriptions as "the way." He proclaims the Kingdom of God, claims to recover the real meanings of the Scriptures, likens the people to sheep, himself to the true shepherd, puts himself in the place of the sin offering and the fruits of the earth, under a new covenant; promises to his followers a fulfillment in the Kingdom of God with victory over sin and death, and soon is put to death as an enemy of society.

His followers see him risen from the dead, accept him as their spiritual food, and memorialize God for him as their real sacrifice. They believe that the same Spirit who ordered the chaos in Genesis, makes the crops fruitful, and gave the prophets their divine messages also caused the birth of this Jesus, and showed forth the power of God both through him and through them. They are united in this life through a Church which inherits the vocation of Israel under the new covenant. So much for the Bible themes.

This new-covenant religion made its way against odds. It was cast out as a heresy by the followers of the original covenant and spasmodically suppressed by the Roman authorities. Moreover the competition in the ancient world with other salvation religions and salvation philosophies was a lively one, in which only the most vigorous survived. The two "covenant" religions and the stoic philosophy were the principal survivors, but the religion of the new covenant did more than survive. It far outstripped all others in missionary zeal and success until it took over the western world, turned against the followers of the old covenant, and forced stoicism to blend with it.

We Christians know the corruptions into which our religion has fallen. We know, with shame, the godlessness of the Church of God, but we also believe that the judgment which God himself visits upon the Church does not keep it still from being the Church of the New Covenant.

What have we done with the Bible themes? Out of a plush tradition, managing its own salvation, we have used them as romantic escapes. The God who is, has become the God whom my best self creates. He is now a product of my thoughts instead of my being a product of his thought. Moreover, since my thought cannot achieve any such product, this God must be kept subtly away from the activity of thought; so we sing about him in hymns, instead. The act of belief is no longer an act associated with any conviction within me. It is merely a device whereby I cling to the feeling that life is, by nature, beautiful.

Because we have so grossly transformed the Bible themes to conform to a self-saving society, we no longer remember what those themes really are. As our community life is forced to give up its illusions, to use shock language, to submit to force and to a growing cynicism, we have the mistaken impression that we are losing our religion. As a matter of fact we didn't, as a community, really have the religion. What we are losing is the cult of a romanticized Jesus.

It may seem that the distance by which the Bible is removed from us in time, culture, and scientific knowledge has weakened its authority. However, the Bible's belief that the ultimate origin of all things is God touches that area of ultimates which no extension of our knowledge can reach. Scientific knowledge cannot dispense with an assumed starting point, so that the choice of belief is always open. Apart from the question of origins, the Bible's description of the physical world has been displaced by an immeasurably awesome universe. If the Bible did not boast so much about what God can do, this might be embarrassing, but as it is, our new astronomical knowledge shows the boast fulfilled better than the Bible writers themselves imagined.

With regard to the cultural colorations of the ancient Semitic world which are strange to us, we must remember that the differences in political and religious behavior are not so extreme as we thought. The brutality of our politics and the corruption of our religious life are close to matching their Biblical counterparts. Where there is a real difference between the Bible's Oriental outlook and ours, it is enough to point out that the Bible is not important for the ingredients which it shares with the *Arabian Nights*. It is important for the ingredient by which it differs, namely, its statement of God.

We should learn a lesson from the very manner in which the Bible makes this statement. The fact that the settings in which it places the statement are so bloody, uninspiring, hateful, disheartening, and factual should make it clear that this God is not the product of an ideal society. He is a God who speaks, through his own, to a corrupt society. The fact that the new-covenant story contains the death, at the hands of the religious community itself, of its own best exemplar, should teach us that this God does not "play it safe" but continues to run the highest of all risks.

These clues restore to our view a Christianity which has sources deeper than the social trends. Its God is Alpha and Omega, the beginning and the ending. If our society is growing more impious, the Bible is an impious book. If honesty is not the best policy, it is still a requirement of God. If storms are destroying the spiritual houses of our contemporaries, the house built by Jesus' specifications is established upon a rock. If pious belief is losing ground, another kind of belief is responding to tangible invitations from the God who is. If tradition looks stuffy from the outside, its contents, appropriated from the inside, are a frontier experience full of agony, danger, death, and abundant life.

EPILOGUE

And when he drew near and saw the city he wept over it, saying, "Would that even today you knew the things that make for peace! But now they are hid from your eyes. For the days shall come upon you, when your enemies will cast up a bank about you and surround you, and hem you in on every side, and dash you to the ground, you and your children within you, and they will not leave one stone upon another in you; because you did not know the time of your visitation."

And he entered the temple and began to drive out those who sold, saying to them, "It is written, 'My house shall be a house of prayer'; but you have made it a den of robbers." [1]

This passage epitomizes Jesus' watchmanship. It underlines his warning to the community and his cleansing of the Church. He is presented here as a lonely figure, but not lonely through lack of participation in the life of his day. He was lonely because the community rejected him, and he, for his part, rejected the unholy practices of the temple.

Yet his loneliness among men was only partial, for the story goes on to tell how those who sought to destroy him "did not find anything they could do, for all the people hung upon his

[1] Luke 19:41–46.

words." [2] So, while he was not a successful man communitywise, he was the people's man.

This is a dangerous phrase to use, "the people's man," because it describes the demagogue and sometimes the leader of sedition. In what way was Jesus not a demagogue and not a leader of sedition? He was not these things because he had given himself, his talents and his love of life, over to God. Therefore, when God gave them back to him to enjoy, they functioned in God's way, that is, to the benefit of others. The tree was good. Therefore its fruit was good.

Today's watchman is in an impossible situation if he approaches his watchmanship with nothing more than the virtues of the community to guide him. If he is to see what the community does not see, he must himself be a God-guided person and not just a community-guided person. The work of prayer and the pain of isolation are two aspects of the price he must pay.

Yet he must also be a participant in the events of his day. He is himself a sinner. His apartness is that which comes from seeking God. It is not that which supposes that he is possessed of superior virtue. He must also be a participant because his own talents cannot be purified if they are allowed to decay in idleness. The purification of his talents is accomplished not through inactivity but through turning them over to God, through giving up the demands of self, through the losing of one's life in order to find it again.

Out of that preparation comes the watchman's tower, the symbol of the clarity of his vision, something very different from the "ivory tower" of the withdrawn theorist. Equipped with soundness of eye, he has things to say when God is ready to have

[2] *Ibid.* 48.

him say them. Of himself, he will not always want to say them, because he does not enjoy finding fault nor running the risk of loneliness. Furthermore, some of the things God gives him to say will seem to him too obvious. He will forget, at times, how characteristic it is of human society to build success by concealing the obvious, and therefore how necessary and dangerous it is to point out the obvious.

These experiences and many more will be his lot. Unlike his general position among the clergy, and unlike the professional positions of doctors, lawyers, and engineers, his position as a watchman is not sustained by an organization of watchmen meeting once a month. His watchmanship will be his alone, given to him by God. Like all others of God's gifts, that given to the watchman will have in it something unique, which even his fellow watchmen cannot share nor help him with. It is perhaps a sign of the jealousy as well as the glory of God that no one made in His image will exactly match anyone else.

As the tree is made good, its fruit will become good. The things which God's watchman sees and reveals in the life of the community will cause him to be rejected, but time will show that he spoke the truth; and what he does in the Church will cleanse it. Finally, the people not blinded by the world's success, who know they are confused, will hang upon his words.